# Copyright Notice



# Publisher's Notice

*Published by*
*Lesley the Writer Publications*
*4142 Ogletown-Stanton Rd. #442*
*Newark, Delaware 19713*

*First edition: July 2009*

*Visit our website at www.LesleyTheWriter.com*

*ISBN-10: 1-931450-00-5*
*ISBN-13: 978-1-931450-00-3*

# Table of Contents

*– ON YOUR MARK… –*



*– GET SET… –*



*– GO! –*

## – GET TO THE FINISH LINE –



## – MAKE YOUR VICTORY LAP –

# Instructor-Led Class Availability

Lesley the Web Resource, LLC is committed to helping people help themselves.

The concepts in this manual are basic and extensive. However, we offer website design workshops that are even more basic.

If you would like to schedule a basic website design workshop, please contact Lesley the Web Resource, LLC at 302.292.1717.

Simply let us know how many will be attending, so that we know how many manuals you will purchase as a gift of extended learning from you to your participants. Discounts are available for volume purchases.

# Volume Discount Purchases

Please note that the following discounts are subject to change. Make sure you are on the list to receive updates to this manual.

| Quantity of Manuals to Purchase | Price Per Manual | Discount |
|---|---|---|
| 1 – 4 | $49.95 each | 0% |
| 5 – 19 | $44.95 each | 10% |
| 20+ | $39.95 each | 20% |

NOTE:

If you have purchased this book through an online bookstore, you must send us proof of your purchase (e.g., purchaser's email address, mailing address, confirmation number, etc.) so that we may verify the quantity purchased through one transaction. If you qualify, we will send you a rebate check by mail. Mail proof of purchase to: Lesley the Web Resource, 4142 Ogletown-Stanton Rd. #442, Newark, DE 19713.

# Advertise in the Q.U.I.C.K. Fix

Advertise your business within the manuals requested for our instructor-led classes.

Advertising rate is currently $600 per 50 manuals, as space is available, 50-manual increments.

Rates are subject to change without notice, so please inquire about advertising in the Q.U.I.C.K. Fix by calling 302.292.1717 today.

# Q.U.I.C.K. Fix Legend

## Terminology

We have separated terms which we believe are necessary for you to grasp the very basic concepts outlined in this manual. When you come across such terms, notice the underline and look for the symbol to the left.

## Trixy B. Quick

Trixy is your journey mate. She, like you, wants to design a basic website the Q.U.I.C.K. way. When it is time to apply website design knowledge, you will notice the symbol to the left. That's Trixy's subtle hint that it's time for hands-on web design.

## Computer Code Puzzle Piece

Trixy will introduce you to applying the basic website design method, but you can try things on your own, too. Just look for the puzzle piece, like the one on the left.

# .1.
# Take Control of Your Website Design

## Website Design Myths and Misconceptions

Money can be a driving force for business decisions, and personal decisions, too. In fact, people tend to have an apprehension that they will not get what they pay for when they select a service provider. This attitude is at the heart of why many of you may be untrusting about having a professional take over your web design.

The biggest myth is that the professional is out for your money. Professionals deserve to get paid for their expertise and training. You may have felt like you were cheated of your money or your time because you didn't really have a professional at all, or because the professional you worked with specialized in an area not relevant to the scope of your project.

The second biggest myth is that the professional will take forever to get things done. Good web design takes time. Even marginal web design takes time. Either you will take the time yourself or you can leave it to a trained professional who knows best how to spend the time given.

The third biggest myth is that, after all of that time and money, you still won't have the web design that you want or need. You will get the web design you need as long as you keep the lines of communication open. Be honest about what you want and the means with which you have to make it happen. If you are gutsy enough, you can do it yourself. When you feel it is time to call in a professional, check out the resources in the back of this manual.

## Why You Require a Website

Communication to your circles of influence is made easier and faster via the world wide web. Your website is the way to make that connection happen today. Think of your website as an extension of you. Individuals are able to use a website for anything from a personal blog to a personal following, like a book author would have. Businesses can use a website for anything from selling goods or services online to communicating information with its sales force.

Websites should no longer be thought of as an option. It is a necessity for anyone who has someone or some group with whom to communicate. It is simply the fastest mode of mass visible and audible communication. Don't make the mistake of skipping over an opportunity to share yourself more quickly within your circles of influence. You have already made the first step.

## Missing: Your Business Website

Impressions start with first sight. If you, as a business owner in today's world, do not have a website, it is tantamount to being a realtor without a car. It is unnatural, to say the least. It is also old-fashioned. Many years ago, a one-person business could get away with a numbered post office box, a few business cards, and a phone number. That would have been enough to have an acceptable business appearance. Now, you must also have a website as a bare minimum. What you use that website for is altogether up to you, and we will cover the purpose of your website soon within the pages of this manual.

For now, it is most important to realize that a website can do so many things for you, the most important of which is to increase your business presence in the world. However, simply owning a website is not enough.

## Poorly Designed Websites and People Who Own Them

Perception is a large part of attracting customers for your business. Imagine if you were to visit an unprofessional website. Would you give your business to someone who cares so little about their website? Perhaps if you yourself cared little about what the end product or service you received would be, you might be willing to overlook a poorly designed website.

When your customers and potential customers visit your website, greet them with respect by showing that you care about what they think of you. You want them to know immediately that you realize your website is a direct extension of you as a business person. You value their time enough to avoid giving them something of poor quality.

Leave your web visitors with the impression that there are more great things to come. Will your web design change over the next few years, months, or weeks? Yes. Of course it will, just as your business will. However, the thing you want is for your visitors to look forward to coming back. It begins with not putting them off by a poorly designed website.

## Personal Websites Need Attention, Too

Desire and time are two essential elements that you will need to use this manual. Although some of this manual is geared toward the business professional, the realization is that there are various personal uses for having a website, too. This manual is for those individuals as well.

Among business professionals, this manual is for anyone from a one-person business to a business person who has a partner to an individual who works within a slightly larger structure. It is for anyone who has a poorly designed website and who has enough control over that website (by way of access to website files) in order to do something about it.

Among personal users, this manual is for anyone from the individual poet to the new book author with a small following to the head of a social or church group. Anyone with the desire and the motivation to have a website or to fix the website that they already have.

## Ready…Set…Design

Learning web design is not a task for the impatient. It has taken years for me to be able to even explain to you in a simple way the information that is within this manual. Professional web design services exist for the more advanced concepts – concepts that are not going to be covered here. The amount of time it will take you to build or fix your website depends on how much time and patience you have to offer.

Fortunately, in order to use this manual, you do not have to have web design or web development skills. You just need a computer with Internet access (you will learn more about this shortly). Within this guide is access to all of the web design and web development tools you will need to complete the exercises. The skills you will require are the ability to type, the ability to read, and the ability to work patiently within a block of time. You are not even required to know anything about the computer, except how to turn it on and off.

Although the website you will build is basic, this manual is written by a professional for people who are tired of not having a website and for people who realize they need a better website.

## Q.U.I.C.K. Fix Inspiration

2005 was the year I was laid off from my position at a bank, and I have been building websites ever since. I became interested because I wanted to promote my freelance writing talent to a larger base of prospective buyers. Soon enough, I had experience designing small business websites and personal websites. My skill set grew to include more than just web design. I learned quickly how to develop websites, too.

This book is a culmination of those years of experience and experimentation, the very basics of which I have chosen to share with people who may currently be unemployed or unable to work outside of the home.

Knowing that I needed some direction in website design for the writing website I wanted to setup for myself, I looked at various written information. If this book were available when I was starting out, it could have saved me a lot of computer viruses. I even researched book stores, but didn't find any that had all that I wanted in one book – and who had the money to buy 10 books at $40 each? Remember I was just laid off at that point.

My determination came through, and little by little I began to realize that my only limitation was my imagination. As long as I had the proper tools for getting my website up on the Internet – a website with code, the desire to make a good impression, and the time and patience to learn – then I could. So I did. Some things are far too complicated to be included in this manual, which is designed as a Q.U.I.C.K. Fix for your ailing (or missing) website. However, it is a great place to start if you want control of your website and your budget.

Control over my monetary budget was what led me to compromise my time in order to learn basic website design. Remember, it was 2005 and I was an unemployed bank representative with a passion for writing. The world didn't exactly know that I was out here, but I learned a couple of years later some techniques (some of which you will learn from this manual) to get some web visitors. I kept writing articles mostly, and kept designing and developing my website until it became what it is today.

Some of you using this manual may now be going through what I did back in 2005. Believe me when I tell you that I know what a monetary budget is. Of course, if you want a more advanced approach, you will seek out a professional which, just like this manual, will be worth every penny you spend once you get more clients or once you reach whatever goal you have set.

## Why Lesley is Okay with Helping You Build a Basic Website

Understand that this manual, though far less than the cost of a professional, is valuable still. I am writing this manual as a professional web designer and developer, and I have gotten to the very essentials of what every person must know in order to make their presence count in the world wide web.

If it makes you feel any better about the value of this manual, look at the price tag. Even if you were graciously given a copy as a complimentary gift, the value contained within is immeasurable. If you are the person who has no website, but needs one, this is your manual. If you are the person who has a poorly designed website, this is your manual. If you are like I was and want to take more control of your website, this is the manual for you.

## Q.U.I.C.K. Fix Manual versus Seemingly Similar Books

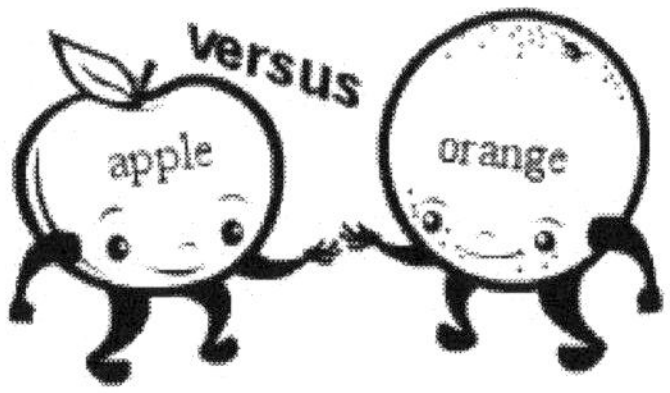


Simple and easy-to-understand definitions and examples fill this manual from cover to cover. Unlike some books out there, this book gets directly to the information without too much extra information that you will not use for your immediate remedy. This book is a complete and Q.U.I.C.K. Fix to your ailing or missing website. It is not a book at all – it is a self-paced learning manual. Each example is quick. Each definition is quick. The Q.U.I.C.K. method is quick. If you were to spend about 90 minutes on each example you will be well on your way to fixing your website or building your website quickly. You can start from absolutely nothing – no knowledge of websites and what it takes to build – to having your quality website up in a matter of days.

This complete guide is as simple as the bigger books that are also not complex, but it gets right to the problem and offers the Q.U.I.C.K. Fix. No messing around and giving you far more information than you will need. I want you to keep this guide as a tool, not as something which will collect dust on your bookshelf.

## Website Owners and Would-Be Website Owners

Attitude is everything when it comes to learning. Whether you are learning something for the first time, or trying to build on what you may have learned a while ago and cannot remember. If you possess the correct attitude, this book will give you the ability. You will not become the city's best web designer by using this manual. However, if you purchased this manual, that is not your intent anyway. Your intent is to fix a website that needs to be fixed. Similarly, you may want to invest time in getting a website for personal or business use, and you want to present yourself in the best possible light.

This manual is for those people, young and not so young, who realize the value of a first impression. This manual is for those people, business and personal, who realize that a web presence is a necessary mode of communication at some juncture of their life. This manual is for those people, experienced with computers and not experienced, who have the ability to read, type, and work through the provided examples. It is for the patient person who may not possess web design experience but who possess the skill set (mentioned above) to take on this task.

## Start Learning Today

Access to a computer and blocks of time are required. If you do not have your own computer, you may be able to use a community computer. For example, the local library usually has computers available by allotment of time. Ask for the sign up sheet to reserve your time. Even if you can only use a public computer for a small amount of time, you should be able to work on this task with relative ease.

Of course, public computers have one limitation – you may not be able to get photo images to use (as you will be taught soon). Another possible limitation, though rare in this day and age, is that the public computer may not have internet access, which you will need once it comes time to getting a domain name, hosting your website, and making your pages available for the world wide web to view. Be sure to check the restrictions of computer use at your community facility.

Clear out time in your day to dedicate to the task of building or fixing your website. Armed with a computer that has internet access and your patience and desire to learn, you are well on your way to building or fixing your website with the Q.U.I.C.K. Fix.

## Solutions Uncovered in This Q.U.I.C.K. Fix Manual

Basic web design and development concepts are covered in this manual. There are times when the example will leave many questions in your mind as to what else you may be able to do if only you had more information. Imagining the possibilities is part of the beauty of this manual.

Take your time with the lessons, and get to know why certain web design and development parts work the way they do. If you grasp the inner workings of the code, you will be pleasantly surprised at the number of possibilities that await you. To reign it all in, occasionally I will remind you that this manual is a Q.U.I.C.K Fix, and the goal is for you to come away with a basic website – and a complete website.

Tools included in this manual range from web design definitions to full-blown examples. You will journey with Trixy B. Quick as she builds her website from scratch. You will help her realize her dream of owning a basic, yet professional, website. You will learn about the Internet and basic Internet terminology, about domain names, and about choosing a website host. You will learn how to code in order to tell your computer what type of website you want communicated via world wide web. Most importantly you will have a basic and complete website.

# .2.
# Internet Past, Internet Present

## Your Place in the World Wide Web

Communication can take place in various ways. Basic elements include a sender, a message, and a receiver. Simple right? Regardless of what type of communication you engage in, the three elements are present. The face of communication was forever changed with the introduction of the

Internet and the method of connecting to the Internet in order to read and write information to the world wide web. It became faster to communicate with people around the world. In fact, the world wide web came about as a result of a need for linking database pages.

*Internet*
*a global network that connects computers*

*world wide web*
*a set of documents residing on the Internet*

When you turn on your computer and use your Internet service provider to visit your favorite search engine (your portal to all the information available online), search results will bring up a description complete with a domain name after domain name. Each of these domain names will most likely begin with www – which stands for world wide web. Keep in mind that there are quite literally millions of these domain names across the world wide web. Plenty of websites from which to choose to pull the information you seek. Your goal is to be one of these websites.

## History of the Internet

An evolution of computer networking, mostly for government purposes, led to the Internet – a protocol for computer information sharing. In the 1980's, an English computer scientist named Tim Berners-Lee formulated the hypertext and hyperlink mechanisms that are the foundation of the world wide web as we know it. Just like most things, necessity brought about the ideas for the computer, the Internet, and the world wide web. The rest is history, and history is unfolding as we speak.

## Get Connected

By the late 1980's, the private sector – people like you and me – had a way to connect to the Internet by using an Internet Service Provider (ISP). Nowadays, there are several from which to choose – some offer more features than others, and some will be bundled with other communications services. There are hundreds based in the United States of America alone, so imagine how many there are worldwide. As you search for your ISP, you may want to consider asking your friends and family which ISP each of them uses and if they are happy with their choice.

## Dawning of the New

Improvements include the speed at which we can access the Internet. The dial-up method, where your computer would literally dial a phone number like you would call a friend, was how we initially gained access to the Internet. Cable connection led to access speeds unheard of in the late 1980's.

Another major improvement includes the amount of security. The world wide web is a haven for high-tech thieves and other criminals. Since the early 1990's, with the introduction of the secured socket layer, the Internet has had a few improvements security-wise. However, you should remain as cautious as possible when surfing and using the world wide web.

*surfing*
*moving from place to place on the Internet*

Growth of the Internet being what it is, there are sure to be further improvements. Just be certain that you do what you can to keep yourself informed of the changes which may affect the way you search and conduct business and personal affairs online.

## People Who Use the Internet

According to the Internet Statistics: Usage and Population Statistics 2008 census, there was an estimated 1.6 billion Internet users worldwide[1]. This is an Internet generation. I remember a very basic computer class being an option (not a requirement) in school high school when non-government folks were just beginning to gain access to the Internet. The class I elected to take wasn't even the easy-to-use windows-based classes of today, but the tedious coding classes where we had to use a DOS prompt to communicate commands to a computer. Now, I believe babies are born with a computer keyboard in one hand and an Internet cable in the other.

*online*
*connected to a computer service through a piece of equipment called a modem, in the case of being connected to the Internet*

*windows-based*
*Microsoft Windows family of operating systems*

*DOS*
*disk operating system; an old operating system that provides the base for many computer application programs, and still operates behind many newer operating systems*

*browsing*
*same as surfing, in this case*

Research is a great part of the Internet, but people use it for more than browsing. Families can find entertainment, like legitimate music downloads for iPods and mP3 players and DVD rentals. Parents can find coupons (and stores) that may not be available to them otherwise, and they can pay bills online as well as access work from home. There are many opportunities to use the Internet for common purposes. Information is conveniently exchanged on the Internet via the world wide web, and users – like the ones you hope to attract by building or fixing your website – look for that information every day.

## Websites, Design, and Development...Oh, My!

Exchange of information that you see on the Internet is done through websites. When you access the Internet, you are viewing the website through a web browser. You may have Internet Explorer or Fire Fox, but there are others, too. When you search from the browser for the information you need, you are given a number of domain names, which will lead you to respective websites. When you complete this manual, you will have your first website or you will improve the website you have. A website is what contains the information you wish to be publicly available to the world.

*websites*
*a location (site) on the world wide web; contains at least one web page*

*domain name*
*provides a label for (and a link to) a given website*

*web page*
*a document on the world wide web*

*web browser*
*often called browser; an application used to locate and display web pages on the world wide web or on private networks*

A website page (or web page) is information which you can view without the name in the web browser changing. For example if you visit, www.DesignMyOwnWebPage.info, you will see a web page, the home page. If you click the link that says resources, you will be taken to a different page. A web page can be as long or as wide as you want. However, for one key reason, which we will discuss later, you should use care when deciding how long to make your web page.

*website designer helps you determine the page layout, graphics, text location and website colors, as well as navigation across your website*

A website is made up of as many web pages as you have associated with one domain name. In the example above, the home page and the resources page make up the whole website. Many people use websites for many reasons, including research, transactions, entertainment. Can you think of anyone who would want more information on something for a book report or a business proposal? Can you think of anyone who might want to pay their bills online or access their work files from home? Can you think of anyone who may want to shop from the convenience of their home for everything from bananas to boots? Now imagine that you, the business owner, has a service or product related to these consumer needs for using the Internet.

Perhaps you have a business proposal writing service or maybe you sell business proposal presentation materials at half the price of most office supply shops. Maybe you have a clothing or specialty foods shop. The point is that both consumers and providers need the Internet. As the service or product provider, you have this manual because you want your website to positively stand out as much as possible.

Color and style for a website are important. A professional website designer can work with you to unlock the best uses of style and color for your website. There are blended variables that you will consider within this manual to make your website the one that a potential buyer wishes he or she had found hours ago when searching for lizard knick-knacks or whatever you are selling. Your website will be reflective of the image you wish to portray via the world wide web.

Present what you have to present in the best way possible for the amount of money and time you have to invest. If you have all the time in the world and are short on skills, this manual will give you the bare essentials, and more information on what else to consider, for designing the website worthy of your business (or personal) image. If you have little time or little imagination, leave it to a professional web designer. She will be certain to take into account what your needs (and your target audience needs) are. If you also require website development, be certain to research your options in order to find a professional that can handle your web design *and* development needs.

*target audience*
*primary group of people to whom a product or service appeals*

*website developer*
*programs the functionality of a website according to your needs*

Interesting websites usually begin with a good design, something that captures the web visitor's eye long enough for them to at least consider sticking around to read more or find out more about your product or service. How do you get the web visitor to stay a little longer? Add a dash of functionality and/or interactivity. Give your visitors something relevant to do. If your website is about monkeys, let your web visitor hear the call of different types of monkeys from around the world. If your website is about mortgages, have a mortgage calculator on your website for your visitor to use. These are two advanced examples, which should be taken to your nearest professional website developer so she can work out the details for developing the website of your dreams.
Interact with your visitors, too. Say hello in a different language based on the day of the week, or have the background color change according to what the Internet user tells your website they want to see. These are two advanced examples of interactivity, which should be taken to your nearest professional website developer so she can work out the details for developing the website of your dreams. In the meanwhile, you have in your hands my Q.U.I.C.K. Fix, which will give you a couple of very basic development and interactivity tools for your website.

## Your Reputation Comes First

As a person who entertains business or who is thinking about entertaining business, you must realize that people will begin to know your reputation before you get a chance to introduce yourself. This will happen because you will have done business for Mrs. Parker, who has told all of her book club friends what a wonderful job you've done on installing her marble floors. Mr. Jeffries – an avid reader who joined the book club last year – told his son about you because his son and daughter-in-law have purchased their first billion-dollar home. Mr. Jeffries heard that you have the Italian tile that his son has always wanted and you can install it more quickly than anyone else in the area. And so on and so on.

Why would you want your website to fail you after an introduction like that?

Suppose your tiling business is so popular that you need your website largely to take initial inquiries for you. If you have an awful website – one that has no purpose, no interest, no functionality or interactivity, unorganized content, and no visitors – you are doing yourself and your business a disservice. No matter how great a job you do, regardless of how great a product or service you have, if you lead someone to an awful website, you may never hear from them again.

## Today Is That Day

Planning for your business and budgeting for expenses is no easy task. You must make important decisions like choosing a business name, business type, hours of operation, method of operation, product or service line, etc. Just as important is how you will market your business. In my opinion, the best time to think about getting a website is from the very beginning of your business planning. If you already have a business, then start thinking about a website plan of action when you are reviewing your business plan and goals. It makes it much easier to consider marketing endeavors and what to put on the next thousand business cards and letterhead sheets, and so on.

# .3.
# Q.U.I.C.K. Design

## Q.U.I.C.K. – Method and Benefit

Q.U.I.C.K. is an acronym for the method I have developed to help people have the best website possible. You will learn this method within this manual. Q.U.I.C.K. is also quick – a key benefit to using this manual. You would like a quick fix for your website, or a quick way to get a website up and running. Otherwise you would not have picked up this manual.

Quick is a promise and method all in one. Use this book to get the website worthy of your business. Together we will uncover your Quest, or purpose, for having a website in the first place. We will unlock the Usability and Interest in your website design, and we will create Copywriting worthy of reading. Finally, we will discover the best way to Kickoff your website – new or existing – to announce your new web space via the world wide web.

The Q.U.I.C.K. Fix will help you unlock the Quest-Usability-Interest-Copywriting-Kickoff strategy you will use to get the website you deserve.

## Q is for Quest

Purposeful websites are simply ones that have a reason for being on the web that is larger than just a really neat domain name you have reserved for yourself. For businesses, your Quest can be a way to capture prospective buyers, a special ordering site, a portal for high-end buyers, a meeting place for your sales representatives world wide, a public relations portal, or any number of true reasons your business website will exist. Even if you have settled on operating locally, your business could use a website perhaps to handle your ordering for you, especially if you are a one-person business. It makes sense to have your circles of influence be able to connect with you via the world wide web.

## U is for Usability

Development of your website will make your website visitors want to stick around. This is known as website stickiness. To encourage sticky websites, you can use development tools that range from simple to more complex. A couple of very simple Usability methods are contained within this manual, so we will go through them together. More complex development methods should be handled by a professional website developer. It is important that you develop your website in a way that is appropriate for your audience. For example, you may have seen a really cool mortgage calculator on a website and thought that would be an excellent way to get your web visitors to hang around for a bit on your website. That would be a fact if you had anything to do with buying or selling houses (lender, appraiser, realtor, etc.). If, however, you have a clothing store, you may want to consider some other way to entertain your guests and have them stick around just long enough to buy what you have to sell.

## I is for Interest

Design plays a part in the overall consideration of your website. As your visitors see it, first impression is largely based on your website's design, how attractive it is to view, how easy it is to move around the web page. Add just enough Interest to grab attention, but stay focused on who your audience is. If your audience is a conservative bunch, avoid using busy background patterns and extremely bold color pairings. There are quite a few things a professional website designer can do to help you add interest to your website. There are a couple of simple methods I will cover with you within this manual. You have only about seven seconds to grab their attention. Design your website well and it could lead to your visitors opening up their wallets, or at least planning their return to your website in the near future.

## C is for Copywriting

Typos are bad on paper and on your website. Copywriting (not a typo) is not as easy as it sounds. Website after website is riddled with mistakes or crammed with huge words that nobody understands, sometimes irrelevant words for the chosen topic. Right down to the key words you should consider throughout your text, you should have your thesaurus and dictionary handy for this all-important task. However, you must consider more than just checking spelling and grammar. Careful consideration to how you handle the text within your website could mean the difference between a sale and leading your prospect directly to your competitor's website. As always, when making design decisions like writing copy for your website, keep your target audience in mind.

## K is for Kickoff

Beginning the marketing campaign for your website should always involve consideration for who you want to visit your website. Your target audience is the central reason for everything you plan to design and develop for your website. Since your website is part of your marketing plan, determine the marketing goal for your website based on your website's purpose. For example, if you have determined that your Quest is to have your website be the ordering portal for your widgets, your goal may be to have your website take 50% of the orders. Establishing a measurable goal will help you prepare for your website's Kickoff – even if you are simply redesigning your website. You will have a Kickoff for each new product or service, your latest event, and so on.

## Your Prime Website Real Estate

Focusing on your web page's prime real estate area will save you a lot of time trying to figure out what you want to include on your home page. It will save you time because there is only as much space as you see on your computer screen right now to consider. Realizing that you have about seven seconds to impress a web visitor enough to stick around, and only slightly more time after that to make a buying decision, it makes sense for you to put the information where they can see it immediately. This area is known as your website's prime real estate area. Take care when deciding what to include that you do what you can to match what your target audience expects. If you are catering to dog lovers who are looking for low-cost pet care ideas, it would be best to have a relevant title at the very least as well as a helpful and well-formed menu to lead them to the information they need quickly. All this information should certainly be within reach without having to scroll the page down or over to get to it.

*prime real estate area*
*where your web visitor first looks on your web page*

*home page*
*landing page, first page, index page*

## Q.U.I.C.K. Business

Presentation is everything, especially when it comes to competing for a web visitor's attention. With millions of Internet users, a good portion of whom browse the world wide web daily, you have to do what you can to capture – and hold – their attention. Your number one objective is to make your website worth the time it took for your web visitor to find it. Make it better than the website your target audience visited just a moment ago. Better yet, make it the first – and last – stop on their web journey.

The Q.U.I.C.K. fix for your website is part promise and part method. Promise is in how fast you can use the methods within this manual to fix your existing website or get a new one up and running. Methodology includes gaining an understanding of your Quest, Usability, Interest, Copywriting, and Kickoff elements to design and develop the website of your dreams.

## Q.U.I.C.K. is Quick

Thirteen chapters have specific exercises in them and examples for you to work through. Ninety minutes is the maximum time it should take to review each of those chapters. Existing websites will likely take less time, but a degree of patience is still required. I have written this manual keeping in mind that you are not a professional website designer. This manual is specifically for non-designers who realize the value of having a website. If you multiply 13 chapters by 90 minutes, you will have spent about 20 hands-on hours designing and developing your website. It will be the best 20 hours you could spend on your business.

## Q.U.I.C.K. Examples and Applications

Target audience is certainly an important part of your business website, because without website visitors, your website is merely a place to park a domain name – not much purpose in that. However, even as important as your audience is in the decision of your purposeful website or any other design or development decision, your purpose really boils down to this question: What do you want your website to accomplish? When you have the answer to that, you will know what type of visitors you need to help you meet your goals.

Useful websites certainly cater to your web visitor. You hope that it is useful enough to a would-be prospect, useful enough to have them consider visiting your website again later or telling some other people about it. Regardless of who your target audience is, a useful and free tool will usually hook your web visitor. However, tools deemed valuable to your website visitor do not have to be free. It really depends on your purpose and your target audience.

Style should certainly be considered very seriously. There is nothing wrong with adding a little pizzazz to your website, as long as the type of pizzazz you offer is appropriate for your target audience. Even when you do go a little beyond conservative, especially if your audience is a little beyond conservative, the best websites are the most simply-designed websites. It just makes good sense to have your website be easy to navigate with your eyes, even before you touch your mouse to scroll down or over. Your target audience will appreciate you for it, and they will visit again and again.

So if you are a signage company who is selling signs online, and if you intend to attract people who appreciate artistic signs, the best method for you may be to have your signs scrolling over a faded graffiti. Remember it's okay to get wild with style, but just make it easy for your visitors to navigate and see your pictures with the information to contact you for pricing.

Necessary text is all that is required on your website. Even if your website's Quest is an online newsletter full of discounts for your online shoppers, your text should be exactly relevant to your purpose, and as concise as possible. Make certain that, whatever you do, you recognize the target audience you wish to attract and hold. For example, if you have a website about your traveling hot air balloon ride business, and you want to increase the sales of your highest priced package – sweetheart's sunrise balloon ride – you may want to make sure your newsletter contains romantic language instead of language slanted toward children and how fun it will be. Perhaps emphasize how romantic it will be for the web visitor and his or her spouse, instead. Even though you are going for a certain writing style, keep it short and simple. Remember, you have only about seven seconds to hook your reader – even if your website is clearly a newsletter or a blog. Make sure everything from your title to your picture captions is relevant and concise and driven toward your ultimate goal.

Audience is extremely important in your Kickoff effort. You must get people to your website, so you have several decisions to make when planning your online and offline marketing strategy – regardless of whether you operate only online or only offline or a combination of the two. The response you get to your marketing effort will be well worth it when you make your first sale.

Good kickoff implementations not only consider the audience, but also consider the ultimate goal. Sure, you already have the best wording possible for the online division of your shoe shop – your New Shoe Newsletter website. Now how will you tell your target shopper that the only way to get the greatest discount is through your online division? From business cards to signs, take note of what your buyers responded to when you reached out to them, then repeat repeat repeat.

## Q.U.I.C.K. Words of Advice

Distracting background techniques do nothing to attract a would-be buyer, except in very rare circumstances. For example, having music playing in the background will likely only annoy your web visitor, unless you are an online music-related shop that must have samples of the music you sell. Another example of annoying techniques is an effect that might make the whole computer screen appear to shake or melt or do some other weird thing – unless you have a business specifically catered to cool effects for movies and the like. Besides background distractions, websites that serve no purpose need some Q.U.I.C.K. help. While it is true that Quest is just one of the five elements necessary to employ the Q.U.I.C.K. method, it is the most important. Without a purpose for your website, you are misusing your time. More importantly, without the Q, you couldn't spell Q.U.I.C.K.!

# .4.
# Introducing Trixy B. Quick

## Trixy B. Quick

Years and years ago, Vicky and Micky Quick moved to Slowe City when Trixy was three years young. Trixy was raised among the finest Slowe people ever. She walked track in high school and was on the Slowe track to being the first in her family to go to college. Trixy even went to Slowe City College, where she specialized in Slowe Marketing, a claim to fame of her home town.

Trixy performed remarkably well in college and graduated near the top of her class many years ago. Soon she got top jobs in the health care and travel industries as a top Slowe marketing professional. Over the course of 15 years, she was taking note of what worked well with the outdated Slowe Marketing methods and what could be improved. Recently, she has developed a series based on her new marketing model – Quick Fix Marketing. Trixy wrote several self-paced learning manuals and a lecture series to go along with the manuals. Now all she needed to do was get the word out about her new marketing method and series of manuals and lectures. She decided that she could reach a greater number of people with a website, but she doesn't know the first thing about where to start.

## Trixy Gets a Domain Name for Her Web Space

Trixy B. Quick will discover how to choose the best domain names for her business website. She will find out what key things to look for in a domain name and what to avoid. Trixy will learn how to consider her target audience and her website's purpose when choosing a domain name. She will realize the importance of selecting the correct domain name, and she will discover that it is just as important as choosing the name for her business. You will follow Trixy as she makes her way down a path to a great domain name.

## Trixy Finds a Website Hosting Service

Trixy B. Quick doesn't know much about the Internet or the world wide web, but she will learn why finding the right website hosting company is important. She will learn what bandwidth and disk space are, and she will learn what it takes to get access to her text editor in order to build web pages. She will learn how to upload those web pages to the world wide web. You and Trixy will learn what to do if you already have a web host, and what to do with a domain name you may have purchased but never used. You and Trixy will learn what a parked page is and understand the difference between transferring domain names and changing domain name servers.

## Trixy Learns Basic Website Design Code

Trixy B. Quick is not a website designer, but she will learn basic, easy-to-follow, html tags. You will follow her as she learns some basic web design terminology on her quest to gain Internet presence. She will learn exactly what a tag is, what she should and shouldn't do when using html tags, and more about what it takes to get her website communicated via the world wide web. Trixy will learn about the flexibility of a text editor, how to close and open tags, and what happens if she mistypes the code that builds the website. She will find out what it takes to have others view and enjoy the website she is building.

Considerations for background will entertain Trixy as she discovers what basic options she should consider. She will also find out about things she should avoid when working with background. She will build on her knowledge about html tags in order to start building her own block of background code. Trixy B. Quick will let her imagination run wild, and she will learn to tell the difference between something she can tackle on a basic web design level and things she should leave to a professional web designer.

## Trixy Discovers Color for Her Website

Basic knowledge about color and the web is what Trixy B. Quick will learn as she gets tips on how to make color combinations work for her website. She is not an artist, but she will learn about hot versus cool colors, dramatic versus classic color combinations, and how to get a more sophisticated look. Trixy will get a sample of different color identification methods and how it affects the way she will design her website. She will also learn a trick for adding color quickly.

## Trixy Uncovers More Website Design and Development Code

Building websites can be fun, and Trixy B. Quick has learned quite a bit about the ground-level stuff. Now she is ready to discover the many ways in which text and graphics can be arranged, or laid out, on her web page. She will focus on tables and learn how to consider text and photos within the table. Trixy will build a table for a unique purpose, and you will help her every step of the way. She will learn about linking web pages together and developing her web pages. You will help her implement simple development techniques to increase the chances that web visitors will remain on her website.

## Trixy Gets Website Copywriting Tips

Trixy B. Quick is not a writer, but she will realize the value of following basic guidelines when writing copy for her website. She will learn what to avoid and all of the different copywriting areas there are to consider. She will learn what to include and the best ways to handle copy throughout her website.

## Trixy Plans Her Online and Offline Marketing Strategy

Trixy B. Quick knows that she will have to market – not merely sell – to meet her sales goals for her business. Trixy will learn a few offline strategies to help her target audience find her on the Internet. She will even learn the best online method to help her get website visitors.

## Trixy Learns the Value of a Secure Website

Once she discovers how much it could cost her business not to have it, Trixy B. Quick will learn the very least she can do to protect her website once it is up and running. She will discover the difference between securing her website and securing her computer files. She will discover how her web visitors can tell if her site is safe to use.

## Trixy Gains Knowledge on the Personal Website Q.U.I.C.K. Fix

Similar to the business website she is building, Trixy B. Quick will learn that personal websites are also a reflection of the website owner. She will realize that a decision to build a personal website requires the same Q.U.I.C.K. elements as a business website does. Trixy will discover that there is just as much to consider for a personal website as there is for a business website.

## Trixy Gets Ready for the World Wide Web

Trixy is ready to take the journey and she is hoping that you are ready, too. So far you have learned why your business needs a website, and you know that any business website you own is a reflection of you. You have a fair understanding of the history of the Internet and the world wide web, and you realize that there is room for you in that environment. You have been introduced to the Q.U.I.C.K. method and you realize the importance of your Quest-Usability-Interest-Copywriting-Kickoff strategy in your website planning. You and Trixy have met, and you will become fast friends as you take the basic website design journey together. Your first step is to choose a domain name, as you will learn in the next chapter.

# .5.
# Choose a Domain Name

## The Great Big Deal Over a Little Domain Name

Image is everything. Your domain name is no less important than the name of your business. Your visitors will commit it to memory, if they can. Therefore, if you cannot get a domain name that is your business name, you should take extra care to choose a domain name that is fitting for your business image and your business purpose. Your goal is to choose a name that will attract your target audience. Don't worry. If you have a poor (or missing) domain name, you will come away with a few suggestions here. So let's get started.

## From ISP to Registrar

Connection with the world wide web starts with an Internet Service Provider (ISP). You can do your research to determine which ISP will suit your needs best. In 2005, there were nearly 7,000 providers from which to choose[2]. Even some cable companies offer access to the web, and you may be able to get a discount with a bundle of other services the cable company can offer you. You have choices. Just because you purchase a computer with a free trial to a particular ISP does not mean that you have to use that provider, or stay with that provider if you decide to try them out. If you are basing your decision on price, you will seek out the ISP with the lowest monthly cost. If you are looking for more features in an ISP you will make the appropriate choice.

*Internet Service Provider (ISP)*
*a company that provides access to the internet in exchange for a monthly fee.*

Internet access is the first step toward getting a domain name. Once you get online access, use a search engine and your web browser to get to domain name providers. Whoah! What did I just say? Let us take it one step at a time.

First, you need access to a computer with a modem and access to a phone line (or cable) that is connected to the Internet.

Second, you need an ISP that will either give you software that will allow you to access their systems, or gives you a collection of separate software packages that can be used together. Included in this package most likely will be a browser (e.g., Internet Explorer, FireFox, etc.).

If you do not already have Internet access, you can contact your local library or phone company for recommendations. If you already have Internet access, but want to learn about other access providers, search for another.

There were roughly 1,700 search engines available in 2008[3]. These search engines that have taken the time to gather information on which websites are out there and available for public viewing. Search engines can be small or large. For instance, Google is the largest, followed by Yahoo!, MSN and Ask. You can access these larger search engines by using the search box that you will see on the landing page of the ISP you choose (for example, in the search box you can type ***Yahoo search*** or ***Google search***). If you really wanted to use a particular search engine, you can use your web browser and type in the website address directly (for example, Google.com, Yahoo.com Ask.com).

*search engine*
*a program that searches the world wide web for specified keywords*

*search box*
*a place to enter keywords for search engines to check*

*website address*
*a location on the world wide web*

*registrar*
*has the authority to register domain names*

To get to a registrar to buy your domain name, you can either use your ISPs search box or a search engine's search pages, and type in ***buy domain names***. Typically, ISPs use larger search engines behind their search mechanism. Some domain name registrars are also hosting companies, but just focus for now on getting the domain name you want which is appropriate for your needs.

## The ABCs of Naming Your Web Space

*cyber squatter*
*someone who registers a popular domain name – usually a company name – with the intent of selling it to the highest bidder*

*website traffic*
*amount of users who visit a website*

Choosing a domain name can be a daunting and frustrating task, so I will break it down one step at a time. Before we get too far, understand which characters you can and cannot use. Alphabetical characters and numerical characters can be used within a domain name. The only non-alpha, non-numerical character that is permitted is a dash (-). So you could have a domain name comprised of all numbers or all alphabetical characters or a combination of the two. You could even include one or more dashes (no underscores). Consider carefully before you decide to take such action.

Even though there are only 63 characters permitted, you could come up with many ideas for names that may suit your business needs. Shorter names are better than longer names for many reasons. Shorter names fit better on business cards and other marketing material. Shorter names are easier to commit to memory, both for you and for your target buyer. Shorter names are less likely to be mistyped when typing directly into a web browser or a search engine's search box. Longer names are awkward on business cards, are harder to remember, and are more likely to be mistyped.

It is not always possible to get a shorter name. Shorter names, like acronyms and short one-word websites, are more desirable and have a tendency to be taken quickly, mostly by cyber squatters. Cyber squatters count on the fact that people will want the names that they have purchased and will resell them at a ridiculously high price or not sell them at all, making money from the website traffic drawn to the website because of the name. Often, cyber squatters play with fire by purchasing names of businesses, too. Aside from cyber squatters, some legitimate individuals and companies buy and use extremely popular domain names, and these names are not available for you to purchase. Don't worry...you can still make use of a longer domain name. Remember that the shortest name possible – within your variables – is your goal.

## Find Your Domain Name

**Extensions.** Most people think that you have to use a .com extension to gain recognition on the Internet. There are literally hundreds of extensions out there ranging from .ae to .zm. Some extensions are related to countries, others are related to industries, and still others are reserved for non-profits. There can be various restrictions depending on the extension you use. The easiest to get, for example without restriction, is .com, .info, and .net. It is not entirely necessary to own a .com in order to be recognized on the Internet. There are many other considerations to make when choosing your domain name. A crafty person can find some name that fits their business image and their purpose for having web presence, regardless of which extension they use. In fact, larger companies diversify and use multiple extensions to service their needs.

*extension*
*the last part of a domain name (e.g. in LesleyTheWebResource.com, .com is the domain extension)*

*keyword phrase*
*a phrase or set of keywords used by search engines to look for relevant web pages*

**Try using a generic keyword phrase.** Using a generic search phrase, or keyword phrases, as a domain name, like DesignMyOwnWebPage.info tell the target audience exactly what they will be able to do when they visit the website. It could be a website full of information or products or services to help you design your own website. It would not likely be a business name, and it is longer than desired. However, it is an example of creativity in naming a website space.

**Avoid using a widely recognized trade name.** Legal rights to domain names is a sketchy area. To keep yourself out of trouble, consider three general rules of thumb: a name you actively use in business is okay, same name in a different industry or category okay, your name is okay…generally. Check your local small business association and local business laws or seek the advice of an attorney for more details on deciding on your actual business name. Though the "rules" regarding domain names are less clear, use business naming rules as a guideline.

**Avoid numerical symbols mixed with alpha characters whenever possible.** Sound is different than sight. If you say "one to ten" someone could visualize "1210" or "onetoten" or anything in between. For this reason, unless it is your actual business name, you may want to avoid a domain name with numbers included.

**Avoid double letters and double vowels.** More problems could arise when you try to translate a name from your voice to someone else's interpretation. For example, if you want a website which makes use of a major feature of the one product you sell, it may look like this on paper: Fit Tennis Shoes, may be about the perfect pair of custom made tennis shoes. So you tell someone that your website is FitTennisShoes and the confusion begins. Wherever possible, stay away from double vowels and double letters altogether.

**Try to cover your bases within reason.** If your name is John Doe and you run a bakery with your brothers called Doe Boys. Will your prospect remember that your website is DoughBoys or will they be more likely to try DoeBoys in the web browser? Take no chances...purchase both under whichever extension makes sense to you – if you absolutely must use a difficult-to-translate name.

## Latching Onto a Good Domain Name

Ideas for getting desired domain names include using a subdomain name. A subdomain is a part of another domain name. For example, www.AreaProvider.com is a domain name. If you were to use a subdomain of this website to advertise your business called Flowers, your subdomain name may look like Flowers.AreaProvider.com.

Some website hosts offer free domain names with purchase of their hosting plan. These names are usually (but not always) subdomain names. It is the same concept. Subdomains are also useful mostly if you have a temporary use for your website.

*subdomain name*
*part of a larger domain name*

*website host*
*provides website server space to those who don't have their own*

*parked*
*unused domain names that point to a pre-existing landing page, usually reserved for pay-per-click advertising*

*domain name servers (DNS)*
*translates domain names into IP addresses*

## Park It Right There

Domain names that you do not use will do you no good. Sometimes, as previously mentioned, you will simply get a domain name to cover your bases. When you buy the domain names, you may be automatically set up on the registrar's parked domain name servers. Simply put, domain name servers are what will get your information from the web host to the world wide web. The specific address locations within the world wide web assigned to devices participating in a

*i.p. address*
*an identifier for a device on a suite of Internet communications rules*

*pay-per-click (PPC)*
*a formula used to price online advertisements*

*search engine robots (spiders)*
*a program that follows links throughout the Internet, grabbing content to add to search engine pages*

*WhoIs*
*an Internet tool that returns information about a domain name or IP address*

computer network is known as an i.p. address. When you purchase a domain name, your website will be live to the world wide web, very likely showing many advertisements. Advertisers pay registrars and web hosts a great deal of money to place their ads on parked domain names because advertisers realize that people are looking for something to click, and when they click advertisers get paid. This is known as a pay-per-click website. You can generally register your domain name for any period from one to ten years, which can really mean big bucks for advertisers to win and also big bucks for you to lose if you don't take a moment to design and develop your website for your target prospects to start purchasing your products or services instead of an advertiser's products or services.

## Getting World Wide Web Attention

Registering your domain name is as public as registering a company name to do business within your geographical region (be it county, city, state or country wide). As soon as you register your domain name, there is everything from search engine robots (the electronic mechanism that gathers information for their respective search engines) to cyber squatters trying to gather information on you and your website. There are services available for you to keep your information private from the WhoIs information bank. What privacy registration of a domain name does is give the information of the registrar (the entity that grants you the domain name) in place of the registrant (the purchaser) name. It does not mean at all that they are responsible or liable for what you put on your website.

*registrant*
*a person, company, or entity who owns a domain name*

## Trixy Wants Your Help

Trixy wants to know what domain names you are considering for your business website. That way she will have a good idea of what to call her own. She has registered her name TrixyBQuick.com, but can you tell her the advantages and disadvantages of her decision? Can you tell her the advantages and disadvantages of the other domain name she is considering, now that you know what Trixy's line of business is and who her target market is. Help her according to the suggestions for choosing a domain name outlined in this chapter.

She is considering the following two domain names:

www.TrixyBQuick.com

www.QuickFixMarketingSeries.com

# .6.
# Host Your Website

## What is a web host?

Website hosts (web hosts) have the tools to get your website viewable on the Internet. Immediate access to your website via browsers all over the world starts with your web host. To make your website "live" – available for view and use on the world wide web, you must take a series of actions, including setting your domain name servers, building your web pages, and uploading the files to

*uploading*
*transmitting data from a computer to the Internet*

*publish*
*to transfer web pages to the world wide web*

*bandwidth*
*the amount of traffic that can be transmitted in a fixed amount of time*

*disk space*
*total amount of data that you can store on your web host's server*

*downloadable*
*transferable from Internet to computer*

publish your web pages. There are various web hosts out there, and there are just as many differences between them. It is difficult to compare web hosts on price alone because many of them offer different services in addition to hosting your website. Be certain to get the web host that makes sense for you and your needs.

You can transfer your domain name and your web hosting account to another provider. If you haven't already made the decision as to which web host to use, make note of what you absolutely require in a web host. Do you really need five jillion kilobytes of disk space and bandwidth for your personal website (in a bit you will find out what disk space and bandwidth mean)? Do any web hosts offer a particular service or product that interests you more than what is offered by other providers? Be sure to consider all of your options before choosing one web host versus another.

## Bandwidth versus Disk Space

Bandwidth for your website is typically calculated on a monthly basis. Each of the web pages your visitors view, and every time they visit each of those pages, uses up bandwidth. Disk space is quickly used up when your visitors view your photos, video clips, and downloadable material. Before you sign up with a web host, find out if they will charge you for going over your bandwidth and disk space limit, if there is one associated with your account.

## Choosing Your Website Hosting Service

Look for the following key factors in your web host:

**H**TML editor should be accessible for greater editing control.

**O**ptions should include at least two different hosting plans.

**S**upport should be easily accessible to you when you need it.

**T**erms should be agreeable to you.

**L**ow-cost hosting relative to your needs is a must.

**I**ncremental charge, typically monthly, is convenient and should always be an option.

**K**it for website completion which could include website security and traffic monitoring.

**E**asy-to-use control interface for building your website or making requests of your host.

**L**imit-adjusting bandwidth and disk space, or some alternative to charging for overages on web host's server

**Y**our image and the image and domain name of your web host should match.

*server*
*a device that manages network resources*

Options exist for finding the right web host independent of finding a suitable domain name. If you found your perfect domain name at a registrar which also offers website hosting, you are not obligated to use their web hosting service. You can build and host your website with another service provider. In fact, you can change the domain name servers from the web host where you purchased your names to another web host altogether. Not all web hosts provide domain name purchasing services, and not all providers of domain names offer hosting services. So do your research. If you are looking for a one stop shop, then find a web resource that will give you all of what you need.

## To Transfer or Not to Transfer…That is the Question

*point*
*to redirect*

*propagation*
*the time it takes to send your domain name's address information to name servers across the Internet*

Existing domain names that you purchased at one domain name registrar may be transferred to another. This can be a costly transaction. On the other hand, you can keep your domain name where it is and change the domain name servers. This typically costs nothing and it means that you can buy your domain name at the registrar which is charging the least, then you can point the domain name servers to a website hosting service that offers you all that you need in a web host. Whether you are transferring domain names or simply switching domain name servers, the process is not always immediate.

The quickest way is to choose your domain name servers when you purchase your domain name. The second quickest method is changing it on your parked domain name. The third way is to take your published website offline to change the domain name servers. The third method will take a little longer for propagation – possibly up to 48 hours.

## Host Likely, Most Likely

Examples of fairly simple web design code included in this manual are basic html, CSS, php, JavaScript. HTML and CSS are languages versus code. They describe the format, layout, and structure of text. JavaScript is a client-side script, and php is a server-side script. If your web visitor's browser supports JavaScript, then your web visitor will see your JavaScript development work. If your web host's server supports php (like HostLikely.com does), then your web visitor will see your php development work. If your web visitor's browser interprets CSS and HTML properly, then your web visitors will see your web design work.

*server-side script*
*run from the web server*

*client-side script*
*executed from web visitor's browser*

*text editor*
*a program that enables you to create and edit text files*

## Prepare for a Soft Landing

Your website's landing page is the web page that your target visitor will see first, after they type the name of your website into their browser. Occasionally, you will have updates to make to your home page, but you will need to do this without interrupting the view of your current web page. For that matter, there may be other pages which need updating, too. One way to handle this, without guessing what time your web visitors will be viewing your website, is to publish a work in progress page (we will cover this in a little while). In order to build your page in the first place, you will require access to a text editor.

**Text Editor.** Notepad, found in Windows operating system (click Start Menu then all programs and Notepad), is a text editor. You can also usually find one within your web host account wherever you are able to edit your web pages. Code is most easily seen in the text editor, free of distracting visuals that the WYSIWYG editor gives you. Despite the title, WYSIWYG is not always accurate. So before you publish your pages, use the text editor to manipulate the look of your web page.

*WYSIWYG*
*what-you-see-is-what-you-get editor; not always accurate*

*ftp*
*file transfer protocol; to upload a web page file to a server*

*public_html*
*otherwise known as the root directory; a place to hold web pages to be viewable via the world wide web*

**Publishing Your Pages.** Your website will be live as soon as you publish your files to the world wide web. When you publish, you are uploading or ftp'ing your files. File Type Protocol * (or ftp) historically references computer to computer transfer of files, but has been used since the introduction of the Internet to include uploading files from web host server to the world wide web. All you have to do is sign into your web host account with your supplied username and password, add or edit your pages, and get to an area usually called publish or upload. Anything you publish to your public_html file folder is live to be read via the world wide web.

**Public_HTML.** The public_html is basically your website's gateway to the Internet. The public_html folder is also known as the root (or main) directory. It is identified with a forward slash (/). When you type your website name into your browser, you will see your landing page. You will not automatically see any of your other web pages, unless you (a) typed them into your browser (e.g., www.designmyownwebpage.info/resources.html) or clicked on a link (we will cover this later) within your website.

**Parked Domain Name.** When you buy your domain name, you have two choices: build your web page or to leave your web page in the default setting. Instead of letting the web hosting company take the credit for your website, design at least basic design to get your business the attention it deserves immediately. The very least you can do is build your home page and let your web visitors know when you anticipate your new website will be available. This should encourage them to visit again soon. It all begins with finding a website hosting service to use.

## Trixy Wants Your Help

Trixy wants to go shopping for a website hosting service. She would feel much better if you would take the journey with her.

**Option One**

1. Access the Internet.
2. Search for a website hosting service using a search engine.
3. Research the various options that come up, and sign up for one that suits your needs.
4. Look for instructions on how to point your domain name to your web host's domain name servers.

**Option Two**

1. Access the Internet.
2. Use your web browser to locate www.HostLikely.com.
3. Sign up for the iDesign hosting package.

4. Go to the support pages or await your confirmation email to learn how to use Host Likely's domain name servers.

# .7.
# Basic HTML Tags

## Breaking the Hyper Text Markup Language Barrier

Computers can understand you, as long as you speak their language. Begin to tell your computer what you want to do – beginning with Hyper Text Markup Language, or html. It is simply a way for you to construct your website. If you imagine your hosting account as a neighborhood and your website as your house, then think of html as the slab foundation beneath that house. It is the

*html*
*hyper text markup language; used to create a web page on the world wide web*

*tag*
*a command that specifies how a portion of a document should be formatted*

*html tag*
*a command that specifies how a web page should be formatted for viewing on the world wide web*

foundation on which your house is built. Without html, you wouldn't have much of a website at all. What you don't want is your web host constructing its own house on your property. This is what you bought the manual for, to learn how to build your website home. Make your foundation your own. Build your house the way you want to, and start with speaking html, your computer's language. It's never too late to learn another language.

## Tag…You're It

Commands given to the computer via html will be little more than words on a page without proper structure. You have to put your commands (programming statements) in a way that your computer can understand them, otherwise you will be speaking broken language. Code contained in a tag is what makes sense to your computer. Think of a tag as you playing a game of tag. You tag the computer, and it's the computer's turn to do something. An html tag specifies a command to your computer to build your web page.

**Tag to Open the Door.** At first putting the programming statements (commands) in some logical fashion will take some getting used to, but the end result is well worth the required time, even for a basic website. It begins with opening the tag door. As you have just learned, the concept of html tag blends together two basic definitions – turning hyper text markup language into a block of code that your computer can understand. The < symbol begins the tag, which is only complete when followed by the > symbol. Putting your tag between the < and > symbols is the proper way to open the door (or begin) your block of code.

**Your First Code Word.** Beginning your html code block is fairly simple: you start by opening the html tag door, right? To let your computer know that the language you want to speak is exactly html, just put the language call letters between the < and > symbols at the very top of your text editor file like this:

<html>

Then move directly into the header, like this:

<head>

*head tag*
*defines information like where to find the style, scripts, and title for a web page*

*title tag*
*defines the title of a web page document*

**Head Over to Your Title Tag.** The head tag allows your computer to tell search engines how to handle your web page. The head tag begins the block of code which gives important information about your website to online directories, and the like. Now you are ready to get to the good stuff. The block of code that follows the head tag includes title and meta tag information.

Label your web page with your title tag. It is the very least you can do for yourself as far as online marketing goes. Suppose someone stumbles across your site accidentally and they minimize the web page making it smaller, but they do not close the web page completely. If you had an interesting and relevant title on your page, that title may capture a visitor's attention enough to open it back up and view your website in greater detail. At the very least, search engines will pick up your title information from your head tag and include it in their description of your website. It is the best way to say "hello" via the world wide web. And it only takes a few seconds.

Based on how you learned to start the html tag and the head tag, how do you think you would start the title tag? If you are thinking <title>, you are absolutely right. It is as simple as that, and your block of code will result in a nifty but relevant title. One basic rule of thumb is to keep your web page titles as short as possible because space is limited on the browser bar (top of the browsing window), which is where your title shows up when the web page is open. When the web page is minimized, your title shows up in your computer task bar, which is located along the bottom or side of your computer screen. This is where you may see a clock and your computer's volume control.

**Exercise Your Body Tag.** Body tags define the details of your website. It is the way you want your website to appear to the public – the meat of your website. The body tag door is opened the same way as the other html tags. After you open your body tag door, you paint on your blank canvas. It is almost time to give the Internet something to view (next chapter). But first, learn how to close the doors you opened.

**An Open and Shut Case.** Code blocks contain specific commands for your computer to follow. You already know that when speaking computer coding language, you must open the door. You have learned to make one block of code – a command to let your computer know what title you want associated with your web page. So how do you close the doors and end the blocks of code?

Let us take a look at the following open door tags alone for a moment. We know how to open the door for defining the computer coding language, we know how to open the door for the information at the head of your web page, and we know how to begin the block of code that defines your title:

<html>
<head>
<title>

See if you can figure out how to close the doors by looking at the open door tags together with the close door tags below:

<html>
<head>
<title>
Close My Door!
</title>
</head>
</html>

Did you notice that the close door tags include a slash? Did you notice that the close tags are in the opposite order as the open tags?

**Website House Versus Real House: An Example.** Close the doors you open in your website house as you would in a real house. Imagine yourself coming home from the grocery store with a few boxes of cereal. You ***open the door*** to your house (**<html>**) to enter it. Then you ***open*** one of the top cabinets (**<head>**) to ***put something in*** there (**<title>**), like your boxes of cereal with the labels facing out so you can read them (**the actual title of the web page**). You finally ***finish arranging*** your cereal boxes (**</title>**), and you ***close*** your cabinet (**</head>**). You realize that you wanted to pick up some meat (the body code we will learn later) from the market, so you leave your house, ***closing the door*** behind you (**</html>**).

Basically, proper html form is like walking into a house leaving each door open so that you may exit the same way you came out, closing each door behind you, one by one.

## Tagging Do, Tagging Don't

**You must close what you open**, and you must do that in reverse order. Remember you are walking through your website home, leaving all the doors open until you make your exit. As you exit you want to close all your doors, so this must be in reverse order.

**Use lower-case letters** as shown in the examples and always enclose the open door (beginning) and closed door (ending) html tags in between the < and >.

**Avoid unnecessary spaces.** Basically, stick with Trixy B. Quick, and you will be okay.

## There Are No Surprises Here

You can update your website without interrupting your viewing public's access to it, as long as you wait until you are completely finished before you publish your changes to the affected web page. In order to publish your changes, you must ftp or upload it to your public_html directory, as described earlier. You should not have to change your website in a major way very often. If you do, then you may not have planned your website properly. However, some change will happen, and you will have to handle those changes as they arise, and you can do it without affecting your website. When you do decide to publish your web page to your public_html directory, remember to double-check the look of it in your browser.

**Work In Progress.** Remember your home page is the first page your web visitor will see when typing in your domain name in their browser. You learned earlier that this page is known as the index page. There are other pages to which your visitors will link from your home page. In order to make all of the updating invisible to the Internet, create a temporary page. Even if you are updating a page other than your home page, creating a temporary page to work with is a good idea.

**Expert Typist Need Not Apply.** Errors happen when we are sleepy or typing faster than our brains can process or for any number of reasons. Fortunately, there is a flexibility to simple html programming. If you mistype something, your page will not show up as you intend it, but it is fixable. The key is to view your work – even after you have published it – to see what your visitors will see. Of course, other web design and development languages (other than basic html) may not be so forgiving. You will learn the very basics, here. Remember, this is a complete guide to help you fix your ailing website…the Q.U.I.C.K. way.

## Trixy Wants Your Help

Trixy wants to build her first block of code and add a title to her first website page. She is certain that she will have changes, and she wants to be sure that she knows how to set up a temporary page to use for those changes. She hopes that you will encourage her by building your first block of code and adding a title to your first website page and creating your first temporary page.

*TIP: From your web browser menu bar, select File from the menu, then select New and Window. View your domain name from there, in a separate window.*

**First Block of Code and Title**

1. Access the text editor within your web host. If you are using Windows operating system, you can select Start from your task bar, All Programs, and choose Accessories to access Notepad.
2. Save a blank page as **index.html** by choosing File then Save As and typing the file name into the Save As box.
3. Type the following, replacing "Your Title Here" with the title you want:

```
<html>
<head>
<title>
Your Title Here
</title>
</head>
</html>
```

4. Save again.
5. Look for instructions from your web host to publish your index.html page to your public_html folder.
6. Type your domain name into your browser to view it live.

**Save a Temporary Page**

1. Access your text editor, and open up your index.html page.
2. Save it as index-wip.html, and exit the text editor.

**Host Likely Access to Text Editor**

1. If you use Host Likely, go to Files then Legacy File Manager.
2. Choose Web Root (public_html), then Go.
3. Click the words Create A New File.
4. On the right side, click the down arrow (next to the Create button) to make options appear and select HTML Document.
5. Type in the desired save name, **index.html**, and push Create.
6. On the left side, choose the file you just created by pushing the words.
7. From the right side, choose Edit With Code Editor and select the Edit button that appears at the bottom (scroll) of the next section.
8. Delete all of the text that appears within your editor.
9. Type the following, replacing "Your Title Here" with the title you want:

```
<html>
<head>
<title>
Your Title Here
</title>
</head>
</html>
```

10. Save Changes, and view it live in your browser.

**Save a Temporary Page**

1. Create A New File, as you did above.
2. Name it **index-wip.html**, and Create.

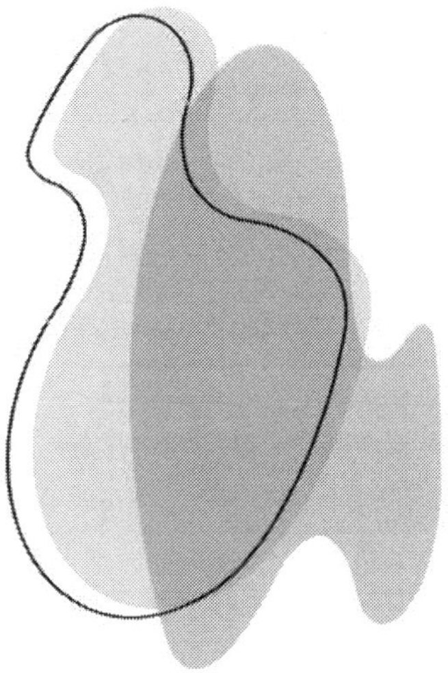

# .8.
# Background Works

## The Fore Front of Design Considerations

If you wanted to add a little pizzazz to your background there are a few ways you can do that. You can alter your background color, background pattern, and background sound. In the next chapter, you will get some suggestions and tips on adding color to your web page. In this chapter, you will learn a few tips about background pattern. Sometimes the simplest method is the best, especially when designing your web page the Q.U.I.C.K. way. The simplest method is to leave your background as it is. The more advanced ways to handle background should be discussed with your professional web designer, who can help you with the effect you desire for your background. Soon you will learn a simple way to add some style to your background.

## Two Magic Background Codes

Color and image codes are what control the background color and pattern effects for your web page. In the following block of code <body bgcolor="FFFFFF">, you are telling your computer what background color to display to viewers (you will learn more about color in a little while). Using the following example block of code <body style="background-image:url('images/b-purpledot.jpg');">, you have specified that you want your background to show an image you have saved in your web files (if you had this image). Don't worry – you will learn more about the parts of specifying which image to use and when later on in this manual. For now, just realize that there is plenty to consider when choosing your background color and image. The top-most concern is to avoid offending your web visitors once they finally find your web page. You should also take care to match the delicate combination of your business image, your personal style, and your target audience preferences.

## Listen Up

Audiences that may appreciate sound in a web page include people looking for music or videos or sound clips from movies. Perhaps even an audience looking for an audio preview of the newest book you have authored. Otherwise, you should probably stay away from using background sound, as it might negatively distract your web visitors. Using purposeful background sound, as mentioned earlier, is a good rule of thumb. Yes, it is a neat feature to have some soft music in the background of a business which deals with romantic candle lit something-or-others, but generally it really is a distracting feature. Just because you can do it does not mean that you should. In fact, there are quite a few people who turn down (or turn off) the volume on their computer because of all of the annoying ads that appear on websites trying to capture their attention. If that says anything at all as to the nuisance brought about by background sounds, I would say that it says to avoid them unless they add to the purpose of your website.

## That's Too Much

Image handling, like all things web designed, can range from simple to complex. For the more complex tasks, like handling more than one image in a background to handling more than one background color, you must seek out a professional web designer who can lend her expertise in that area. Even the least difficult tasks, like handling a single background image can be difficult, especially for those who have had little or no experience in building a web page. This is where the Q.U.I.C.K. Fix comes in handy. Here, you will learn some of the different types of images, disk space considerations, and a simple way to render the image within your background.

## Background Image, If You Please

**Do's and Don'ts.** The value of a background image cannot really be measured. If an image is applied to your background in the proper way, it can add interest to your web page design. If it is done improperly, it can distract people from appreciating the purpose of your web page. Consider image choice, image rendering, and image size. Try to choose an image which accurately tells the story related to your website's purpose. Render your image color intensity so that the attention is not on the background image itself. Size your image appropriately for your web page and your desired effect.

Improperly considering your background image will take the focus away from your website's foreground, on which your web visitor should be focused. You have mere seconds to capture a visitor's attention. Also, including an image (or more than one image) that is large in file size will slow down the loading process, which could turn would-be visitors away due to the amount of time they had to wait for the entire web page to load.

*adware*
*ads that usually popup automatically for people who use free software*

*spyware*
*an application that tracks your surfing habits*

*pop-up ads*
*ads that interrupt your view by opening up a small separate window on your computer*

*cookie*
*a message from a web server to a web browser, mainly to identify users*

**Will Work for Images.** Free sources for images are scattered among world wide web pages. A word of caution about choosing some of the "free" images out there. Some images are free and come complete with adware and spyware and other creepy crawlers that capture your key strokes or make unwanted pop-up ads appear when you search the world wide web. My favorite source is the free images available from Microsoft. They will give you a cookie, and ask you to agree to their download terms, but that's the only price you pay (e.g., no viruses to speak of).

Type **office.microsoft.com** in your browser, and choose the Clip Art button among the tabs that show up on their web page. Ignore the partner sites and ads and focus on the small Clip Art search box with the search button to the immediate right. Search for apple by typing **apple** in the search box and hitting the search button. You will get every free picture related to apples. Leave the word **apple** in the search box, and press the down arrow beside the search button to get a list of available image types. This time choose Photos to narrow your options. You would do a similar search for any photo or clipart you want to use in your website. A word of caution: avoid animations and sounds, as it can get tricky trying to include them within your web page.

Final steps include moving the items you want to your basket by clicking in the open box beneath each picture you want, and choosing Download Item(s) on the left side. Agree to the terms, and that's it. By the way, start with a general search term first, and get more specific if you come up with too many images. For example, searching for people, will bring up hundreds of images. Searching specifically for babies and even narrowing the image type to Clip Art will greatly decrease the number of images for you to a manageable number.

**Locating the Images.** If you have a windows operating system, and you have just downloaded some images, you can find them by using your desktop to access a file folder called My Documents, then go to the My Pictures folder, and finally to the folder named Microsoft Clip Organizer. This is where your images from the free clip art source will be for you to upload later to your web files.

*desktop*
*a system of files on your computer*

## It's All About Your Image

**Photo images** can give a more personal effect. If you are a service provider and you would like to show one person helping another, as you might help someone else, you could use a photo to portray that moment. For instance, if you are a specialty food store, you could locate a cashier smiling and helping a shopper or a produce handler tending to a vegetable stand to convey just the right message for your business. Photos can be altered, but it is a fairly difficult task best left to a professional.

**Cartoon images** or **artistic images** can portray many more informal effects. Usually these images take up less disk space. **Graphic images**, like a single leaf or a water drop, cannot always be easily altered, but they are fantastic for creating patterns. You may be at the mercy of a professional web designer for **custom images**, but the finished product is well worth the wait.

**A Few Good Images.** Graphics are fantastic for holding a web visitor's attention. However, your visitors could pay dearly in the amount of time your web page takes to load. The fewer images the better. If you must have many images, then the smaller in size the better. You may have to seek the advice of a professional web designer to optimize your web page load time. Otherwise, you may find your website visits dwindling as people will not want to return to your website where they will have to wait minutes (versus seconds) for your web page information to load properly. Stick to one photo per every 250 words of copy if possible.

## Background Technique

Techniques available for using a small image for your background include (a) using a single small image, and (b) using a repeat of a small image. Earlier, you learned that using multiple images within a background is best handled by your professional web designer. However, repeating an image is fairly simple. In fact, you have to tell your computer not to repeat the image, otherwise the image you select for your background should automatically repeat. The code for including a non-repeating image is <body style="background-image:url('x'); background-repeat:no-repeat;">, where you would change the x to the name of the image that will be in your web files once you save it there. Trixy B. Quick and you will learn this soon.

Simplicity is key, regardless of what your style is or who your audience is. If you owned an online flower shop, and you found a small icon of two roses tied by a bow, you could possibly use this as a full-blown pattern by repeating the image. If you found that this was too heavy looking because the flowers were too dark or too close together or too anything distracting, you could choose another image.

## Q.U.I.C.K. Designers Don't Need to Edit Images

Patience and experience are really required for editing images. The best method of editing graphic images is to let your friendly professional web designer do the work for you. The important thing to know is that it can be done. You can find the image in advance, or have your professional web designer know what you are looking for, and you can have in mind what you want to do with that image, now that you have learned from this manual some basic possibilities. You really are only limited by your imagination. And if you have little imagination, or need help making your vision a reality, seek out a professional web designer.

## Custom Image Is Not Customary for the Q.U.I.C.K. Designer

Control over your graphic images is probably the lowest item of concern when considering the design of your first web site, or when deciding how to fix your ailing website design. The purpose of this manual is not to make you a professional web designer. It really is to help you fix what you can fix and recognize where others should help you. This manual also will help foster your imagination and bring to you a few possibilities that you may not have thought about previously, possibilities that you can bring to a professional web designer to complete your vision for you. Meanwhile, handle your background the Q.U.I.C.K. way.

## Trixy Wants To Add Style to Her Background

Trixy wants to add a background to her work-in-progress page. Perhaps you would like to do the same. Trixy is going to do the following, and you can try this, too.

1. Get a few images from the suggested free clip art source mentioned in this chapter.
2. Access your web design control panel through your web host account.
3. Access your public_html folder (review Trixy's previous journey).
4. To add the images you just selected, upload the images to your public_html file folder.
5. Open up your index-wip.html file in your text editor (review Trixy's journey).
6. Place your cursor before the </html> in your html code, and press Enter to make a space after the </head> tag.
7. After the </head> tag and before the </html> tag, type the following:

   ```
   <body style="background-image:url('replace');">
   </body>
   ```

8. Rename the x to the one you just uploaded, including the extension. For example, if you uploaded j0441602.png you would type this file name in place of **replace** in the above code.
9. Save changes, and publish your web page according to your web host's instructions.

**Host Likely, an Easy File Upload**

If you are using Host Likely as a web host, here is how to upload your images:

1. Once you are viewing your public_html file folder, select Upload Images.
2. Click one of the Browse buttons, and find the image you downloaded earlier.

3. Click the Upload button once you are finished.
4. Follow the instructions for accessing your index-wip.html page, typing in the code, and replacing **replace** with your newly acquired file.
5. Once you Save Changes, you can view your live web page in another window by typing your domain name and /index-wip.html immediately after your domain name.

Try repeating the image horizontally only:

```
<body style="background-image:url('replace'); background-repeat:repeat-x;">
```

Try repeating the image vertically only:

```
<body style="background-image:url('replace'); background-repeat:repeat-y;">
```

Try using only one instance of the image:

```
<body style="background-image:url('replace'); background-repeat:no-repeat;">
```

# .9.
# Color Vision

## Color Additive

**Background Color.** Stylize your web pages with some color. Color code is fairly easy to add to your website. You could do it the easy way and select a color from the color palette in a WYSIWYG editor. But what fun would that be? My preferred method is through the text editor, which will allow you to see specifically where you are placing your blocks of color code. For background color, you will add the <body bgcolor> tag and follow it with your desired color. Later, you will learn more specifics on how to add color to your background. Now, consider what else you can colorize.

**Foreground Color.** Backgrounds are not the only thing you can alter with color. You can also change the color of your containers (you will learn about containers later). As well, you can colorize your text within your web page. It all begins within the first few lines of your body tags.

## Color Coding

**The HTML Color Coding System.** This color coding system is based on the hexadecimal numeral system. It takes pairs of letters and numbers and strings them together until a block of six digits is formed which control the intensity of color. Color intensity is based on the rgb system, which really takes a look at combinations of Red Blue and Green. For example, #FFFFFF is white because it is taking the highest (or most amount of) intensity of Red (the first pair of F's) Blue (the second pair of F's) and Green (the third pair of F's). If you were to change the F's to all 0's (number zero versus letter O), you will see a black screen because the rgb values are being called at the lowest intensity.

**Color By Name.** Colorizing a web page can be very fun, if only you didn't have to worry about using the hexa-whatchamacallit color coding system. Here's a secret, you really don't for your basic website design schema. You want simpler? You've got it. How about calling up basic colors by name? Try it out later with Trixy B. Quick. I have identified a few colors that you can call up by their basic name, and there may be more. This is certainly a good option for choosing color while you are building, at least to give you a basic idea of what color combinations look like together. If you don't have any colors at all to start with, you can go nuts with experimentation. Here are some colors you can code by their name:

black, blue, gray, green, lightgreen, maroon, navy, olive, orange, pink, purple, red, tan, white, yellow.

## Q.U.I.C.K. Designers Skip Color Matching

Difficulty in matching offline colors to online colors exists largely because of the way that your computer renders the color value so that you can view it. Your computer interprets color from Red Green Blue (rgb), and your printer bases colors on Cyan Magenta Yellow and blacK (CMYK). The best way to handle this problem is not to make it an issue for you. Use colors that are similar enough to your offline marketing material or have your web designer use her expertise at matching colors for you.

## You Can Sing a Rainbow

**Basic Black.** Stylizing with color is definitely fun. Now that you know about what makes up a color, get to the real fun – working out a color schema (set of colors) for your website. There are many colors to consider, but within this manual we will delve into the basic colors and a few extras, starting with the black. Many can argue that black is fairly basic. What you should consider when choosing black as a background color is that perhaps it may better suit one target audience versus others. For example, if you have a website designed for say Halloween or something dreadful that may attract that type of audience, go for it. You could also give a web page with a black background a high end or sophisticated look for selling jewelry, for example. Just think of the dark velvet backgrounds that line pearl necklace cases. Use your imagination and perhaps brighten it up a bit, depending on your audience. White or yellow or orange or light blue text may help with a more sophisticated look, versus dark blue and red which give a more somber color schema.

**Hot Red.** Hot color schemas, like those with a heavy true red background, bring to mind Valentines and something fun. For example, you could style your website with a red background and white text for a website with products for eternal sweethearts, or you could accent your red background with darker text for a high end look. Other factors really play into how your website will be perceived, including the content that is included on your web page. The main takeaway here is that you have to consider your audience and how they may want to view your page. If you have mostly pictures with light background, you could make them pop if you place them on a website page with a red background. Also, you could have the main background be red, and the background of your table, if this is where your text is contained, can be white. This is a splendid way of using contrast to your advantage. And it is merely one of many ways to consider color within your website.

**Vibrant Orange.** Vibrant colors, like orange, is also a great way to bring your pictures to the foreground. What you could do is ask a few people you trust and know that have a want or a need for the service or product you are selling to tell you what they would want in a website that offers that product or service. Regardless of who your audience is, the easier your website is to view the more valuable it will be to your audience. Vibrant colors are inviting, and they can make things pop. With a simple change of text – light versus dark –you can have an outstanding and unobtrusive color schema working for you.

**Warm Yellow.** Happy is what I think of when I see yellow. It is considered a hot color. The darker variations, closer to orange or near a golden type of color, is probably the best option for a table background color. The lighter yellow, like corn meal or butter, are excellent for a whole background. It takes the edge off of the background being completely white, which can strain the eyes when viewing a website page.

**Cool Green.** Cool color schemas, like green, can be useful for various reasons. Cool colors are relaxing and inviting. Cool colors, especially the lighter versions, are soothing and completely unobtrusive. Usually, you will not even have to break up green, for instance, if you intend to use it as a background color. True green, like the color you might see in the basic eight-pack of Crayola Crayons, is an excellent background color for many things, from a money blog to a real estate feature showing. You can be creative, as with all the color schemas, and go light with the text – like the color of butter – for a more dramatic feel, or darker for a more subtle approach. If you choose, you can always break it up and leave some white space within your table containing your text.

**Classic Blue.** Classic blue, like a navy blue, is great for information websites, like a glossary website. Blue is also a cool color, and it is just as inviting as green. The darker the blue, the more inviting it is. The lighter color blue can be more fairy-tale like, depending on the contents within your website, which would depend on the purpose for your website's existence. Blue is not a shocking color at all. Blue, even when darkened to navy for instance, does not have the same effect as black. It is actually quite classic. Go for Americana with a dark blue background, white text container background, and red text or titles. Or simply have a dark blue background and white text for some drama. Use orange, the compliment of blue, over a true blue color for a seriously dramatic website.

**Regal Purple.** Stylizing with purple lends multiple possibilities, too. Purple, a cool color, has a vast amount of possibilities from the fairy-tale feel that comes in using a pastel purple or lavender to the regal feel of using a darker, more majestic purple. For instance, if you have an online mattress store specializing in king-sized beds with a slogan that reads "beds fit for a king", why not choose a royal purple as a backdrop for pictures of these king-sized mattresses? If you wanted less drama, you could have a completely white background and handle your text as royal purple.

**Think Pink.** Many websites do well with pastel colors. Pink, a variation of the hot color red, may fall into the fairy-tale category if it is on the lighter side like cotton candy pink. Hot colors (including pink) may be more for the website that urges a web visitor to act now or forever lose this opportunity to buy your product or service or have your special report emailed to his or her address or whatever else you are urging your web visitor to do. If you have a paint company that specializes in painting beach houses, you could have a bright pink background which might represent the color of a housing project you recently have completed. There are a few possibilities and options for you to consider, if pink is your color of choice. For true pink as an entire web page background, dark text like navy or dark brown work excellently.

**Neutral Brown.** Stylizing with brown shades are fun. You can do anything from very light brown, as in beige, for an unobtrusive, non-white background, to a darker brown to add a more sophisticated look. Brown is an excellent color because it is neutral. Darker brown text over a light brown background is a nice clean look. Dark brown background with light purple or light blue text adds drama. For even more drama, try orange or yellow or white on a dark brown background. As with any color, consider breaking a dark brown background color up even more by adding a table with a lighter background – soft yellow or beige or white – to contain your text. Simply know what you want to accomplish and you will have conquered half of the battle. Take a look around magazines and homes and websites to discover your favorite color combinations.

## Trixy Wants To Colorize Her Background

Trixy wants to change her image background to a background color, and she wants to add some text and colorize it, too. Perhaps you would like to do the same. Trixy is going to do the following, and you can try this, too.

1. Access your index-wip.html file from your text editor (see Trixy's previous journeys).
2. **Important Note:** Trixy's code is getting longer, so she has numbered her coding lines. You do not have to type in the numbers – only the lines of code as one continuous line with no breaks. The numbers indicate each separate line of code.
3. Replace the code that is currently in the text editor, from the <body…> to the </body> tags, with the following code:
    1. <body bgcolor="330033">
    2. <p><font color="lightgreen">Please visit again in one month, when our new website will be available.</font></p>
    3. </body>
4. Publish and view your live web page. Remember, type /index-wip.html immediately after your domain name in order to view your work-in-progress web page.

Find the appropriate lines of code and try the following exercises:

Try changing the color of the text.

Try changing the background color.

Try changing the title of your web page.

Try changing the message to your web viewers.

# .10.
# HTML Table Code

## Contain Yourself

Dividing web page space between your photos and your text can be an easy task with the use of containers. Specifically, tables can enhance the flow of your website, making it easier for your web visitors to follow where you lead them from the title of your article or product information sheet or announcement straight to your sales pitch.

## Setting the Table Tags

Table variables include controlling border thickness or having the borders disappear altogether, paragraph spacing options for handling text within the table, and individual cell background options, like color and image. We will explore each of those table code options here.

**Code Word Table.** To work with table code, start out with <table> which defines the fact that you are getting ready to build a table, then specify your table attributes. Use <tr> which separates each table row, and <td> which has to do with the individual cells within the row. Use <img src...> to add an image to your table. Remember to close your table code by leaving the same way you came in and using your slash before the end tag: </td></tr></table>.

## Trixy Wants To Build Her First Table Container

Trixy is anxious to get her website completed quickly. She senses that you are, too. You and she can get started by accessing your text editor and opening up the index.html file and saving it as index-wip.html, a trick you learned in a previous chapter. Once you have the index-wip.html file before you, type the code Trixy has found (shown below) without the line numbers, one continuous line at a time.

Open your index-wip.html file, and place the following code after the </font></p> tags and before the </body> tag:

1. <p></p>
2. <table bgcolor="white" border="1" width="759">
3. <tr>
4. <td width="245"><img src="greenblink.jpg" width="26" height="26" border="0"></td>
5. <td width="245"> </td>
6. <td width="245"> </td>
7. </tr>
8. <tr>
9. <td width="245"> </td>
10. <td width="245"> </td>
11. <td width="245"> </td>
12. </tr>
13. </table>
14. <p></p>

Remember to replace the image file with one that you have uploaded to your web page files.

Try centering the entire table:

replace

```
<table border="1" width="759">
```

with

```
<table border="1" width="759" align="center">
```

Try adding color to the table background:

replace

```
<table border="1" width="759" align="center">
```

with

```
<table border="1" width="759" align="center" bgcolor="blue">
```

Try adding text to the table:

replace one

```
<td width="245"> </td>
```

with

```
<td width="245">This is some contained text.</td>
```

Try taking away all the table borders:

replace

```
<table border="1" width="759" align="center" bgcolor="white">
```

with

```
<table width="759" align="center" bgcolor="white" cellpadding="0" cellspacing="0">
```

## Resizing Your Table

Code for tables is kind of tricky. If you change the cell width without changing the width of your entire table, you may run into problems; and vice versa. If you change the table width without changing the width of your cells, you may run into problems. For instance, suppose you specified your table width as 600 (which is 600 pixels) and you have a row of three cells at 200 pixels in width each. If you changed the table width to 300, your whole table would get smaller without you updating your cell width. Later, if you decided you wanted to change your cell width to 170, it would appear not to change, and you wouldn't know why. It is because you didn't do your match. To be sure, if you change the width of the table, change the cells in the rows so that the total width of the cells equal the width of the table.

## Table Topics

**There Are Plenty of Tables Available.** Your technique will vary as you determine how exactly you wish to handle the combination of photos and text within your web page. It is acceptable to have more than one table on a web page, which can be as long as you want. Keep in mind your purpose and the audience, and use caution when deciding how much to put on your web page. You can follow one table behind another by simply starting one table code block, adding a few paragraph spacers <p></p> and following that with another table code block.

**Breaking the Table.** A more complicated, but possible format, is to break up a table horizontally. This is truly one large table separated visually by strategic border inclusions to create the effect of a separate table side by side. You may think of a few reasons why you would want to do this.

Flexibility in handling text and graphics is the first thing that comes to my mind. Unless you truly need to break your table up in this manner, stick with the simpler method.

**Table Placement.** Tables are more flexible than they sound. You are not limited in starting tables from the upper left corner of your web page. You may offset your table by several blank entry lines or by several lines of text before you begin your table. You must make the determination as to what is more simple and more visually pleasing and more purposeful for your web design. For example, you could have an article type of website with a miniature calendar right in the middle of the page. You could use a table to contain your text, and creatively arrange the cells so that your text wraps around the smaller table containing a calendar. Imagine the possibilities.

**From the Top.** If you truly wanted to start your table at the top left of your web page, you could expand your opening body tag to include the commands as follows: <body bgcolor="330033" leftmargin="0" marginwidth="0" topmargin="0" marginheight="0">, where the bgcolor would be any color you choose for your background, as described in the chapter on color.

## Trixy Wants To Make a Calendar

Trixy has this wonderful idea to make a calendar, and she wants to create a new web page called **cal.html** to try it out. The following is the code she will use. She has emailed Lesley the Web Resource for the complete calendar code: email@lesleythewebresource.com. If you make a similar page, and name it the way Trixy does, you can view it by typing **/cal.html** immediately after your domain name in your browser.

```
<html>
<head>
<title>Upcoming Events</title>
</head>
<body bgcolor="white" text="black" leftmargin="0" marginwidth="0" topmargin="0" marginheight="0">
<table  bgcolor="white" width="700" align="center" cellpadding="0" cellspacing="0">
<tr height="100">
<td width="816" colspan="7">
<p align="center">January</p>
</td>
</tr>
<tr bgcolor="navy">
<td width="110">
<p align="center"><font color="white">SUN</font></p>
</td>
<td width="110">
<p align="center"><font color="white">MON</font></p>
</td>
<td width="110">
<p align="center"><font color="white">TUE</font></p>
</td>
<td width="110">
<p align="center"><font color="white">WED</font></p>
</td>
<td width="110">
<p align="center"><font color="white">THU</font></p>
</td>
<td width="110">
<p align="center"><font color="white">FRI</font></p>
</td>
<td width="110">
<p align="center"><font color="white">SAT</font></p>
</td>
```

```
</tr>
<tr bgcolor="lightblue">
<td width="110">
<p align="center"> </p>
</td>
<td width="110">
<p align="center">1</p>
</td>
<td width="110">
<p align="center">2</p>
</td>
<td width="110">
<p align="center">3</p>
</td>
<td width="110">
<p align="center">4</p>
</td>
<td width="110">
<p align="center">5</p>
</td>
<td width="110">
<p align="center">6</p>
</td>
</tr>
<tr height="100">
<td width="110">
<p align="center"> </p>
</td>
<td width="110">
<p align="center"> </p>
</td>
<td width="110">
<p align="center"> </p>
</td>
<td width="110">
<p align="center"> </p>
</td>
```

```
<td width="110">
<p align="center"> </p>
</td>
<td width="110">
<p align="center"> </p>
</td>
<td width="110">
<p align="center"> </p>
</td>
</tr>
<tr bgcolor="lightblue">
<td width="110">
<p align="center">7</p>
</td>
<td width="110">
<p align="center">8</p>
</td>
<td width="110">
<p align="center">9</p>
</td>
<td width="110">
<p align="center">10</p>
</td>
<td width="110">
<p align="center">11</p>
</td>
<td width="110">
<p align="center">12</p>
</td>
<td width="110">
<p align="center">13</p>
</td>
</tr>
<tr height="100">
<td width="110">
<p align="center"> </p>
</td>
```

```
<td width="110">
<p align="center"> </p>
</td>
<td width="110">
<p align="center"> </p>
</td>
<td width="110">
<p align="center"> </p>
</td>
<td width="110">
<p align="center"> </p>
</td>
<td width="110">
<p align="center"> </p>
</td>
<td width="110">
<p align="center"> </p>
</td>
</tr>
<tr bgcolor="lightblue">
<td width="110">
<p align="center">14</p>
</td>
<td width="110">
<p align="center">15</p>
</td>
<td width="110">
<p align="center">16</p>
</td>
<td width="110">
<p align="center">17</p>
</td>
<td width="110">
<p align="center">18</p>
</td>
<td width="110">
<p align="center">19</p>
```

```
</td>
<td width="110">
<p align="center">20</p>
</td>
</tr>
<tr height="100">
<td width="110">
<p align="center"> </p>
</td>
<td width="110">
<p align="center"> </p>
</td>
<td width="110">
<p align="center"> </p>
</td>
<td width="110">
<p align="center"> </p>
</td>
<td width="110">
<p align="center"> </p>
</td>
<td width="110">
<p align="center"> </p>
</td>
<td width="110">
<p align="center"> </p>
</td>
</tr>
<tr bgcolor="lightblue">
<td width="110">
<p align="center">21</p>
</td>
<td width="110">
<p align="center">22</p>
</td>
<td width="110">
<p align="center">23</p>
```

```
</td>
<td width="110">
<p align="center">24</p>
</td>
<td width="110">
<p align="center">25</p>
</td>
<td width="110">
<p align="center">26</p>
</td>
<td width="110">
<p align="center">27</p>
</td>
</tr>
<tr height="100">
<td width="110">
<p align="center"> </p>
</td>
<td width="110">
<p align="center"> </p>
</td>
<td width="110">
<p align="center"> </p>
</td>
<td width="110">
<p align="center"> </p>
</td>
<td width="110">
<p align="center"> </p>
</td>
<td width="110">
<p align="center"> </p>
</td>
<td width="110">
<p align="center"> </p>
</td>
</tr>
```

```
<tr bgcolor="lightblue">
<td width="110">
<p align="center">28</p>
</td>
<td width="110">
<p align="center">29</p>
</td>
<td width="110">
<p align="center">30</p>
</td>
<td width="110">
<p align="center">31</p>
</td>
<td width="110">
<p align="center"> </p>
</td>
<td width="110">
<p align="center"> </p>
</td>
<td width="110">
<p align="center"> </p>
</td>
</tr>
<tr height="100">
<td width="110">
<p align="center"> </p>
</td>
<td width="110">
<p align="center"> </p>
</td>
<td width="110">
<p align="center"> </p>
</td>
<td width="110">
<p align="center"> </p>
</td>
<td width="110">
```

```
<p align="center"> </p>
</td>
<td width="110">
<p align="center"> </p>
</td>
<td width="110">
<p align="center"> </p>
</td>
</tr>
</table>
<p> </p>
</body>
</html>
```

Try your own color combinations. For instance, replace

```
<tr bgcolor="lightblue">
```

with

```
<tr bgcolor="yellow">
```

Try adding borders to one cell, and more if you like:

replace

```
<td width="110">
```

with

```
<td width="110" style="border-width:1; border-color:gray; border-style:solid;">
```

Try making the calendar the correct month and the correct year.

Try making multiple pages, one for each remaining month of this year.

# .11.
# Designing Your Personal Website

## Q.U.I.C.K. – Method and Benefit

Q.U.I.C.K. is an acronym for the method I have developed to help people have the best website possible. You have been learning this method within this manual. Although we have talked about your business, you can also use this method as you uncover your Quest, or purpose, for having a website in the first place. You can unlock the Usability and Interest in your website design, and you can create Copywriting worthy of reading. Finally, you can discover the best way to Kickoff your website – new or existing – to announce your new web space via the world wide web.

As a personal website owner, versus a business website, your Q.U.I.C.K. considerations will be slightly different. However, they are all still applicable to your website. We will explore what each of the elements are as they pertain to your personal website. The Q.U.I.C.K. Fix for your personal website is to unlock the Quest-Usability-Interest-Copywriting-Kickoff strategy you will employ to have the website you deserve.

## Q is Still for Quest

Personal websites are usually not maintained for the purpose of gaining money. However, there are a few instances where this may be the case. Consider, for example, if you are a new book author and you want to foster your book sales by letting everyone know, in the quickest way possible, that you have a self-published book for sale. What better way is there than a personal website? Why do I say personal versus business? Isn't anything that references taking in money for service or product considered business? Yes, the act is business, but as an author (and a select few other such occupations), you may not treat it as a business, exactly. You may freelance your services or something of that nature. Nothing is meant to slight the hard work required of an author to sell his or her novel, but the Quest for such a website will be different than say the purpose of a book publishing house, whose business website may be used to fulfill orders of that same book in large quantities.

## U is Still for Usability

Personal websites still require an element of Usability to them in order to encourage web visitors to stick around, whether the website is for listing a set of poems or whether the website is for selling a chapbook (book of poems). For instance, a web visitor to your book promotion website may want to be able to preview a select chapter or the table of contents or the front or back cover, similar to what Amazon does to promote their books online. Whatever your personal website's Usability feature is, consider who your target audience is first.

For personal and business websites, the main focus must be your target audience, if you hope to maintain a successful presence on the world wide web. There are many ways to develop your personal website in order to consider Usability, from simple to complex, some of which were explored in this manual.

## I is Still for Interest

Interesting personal websites are pivotal in gaining worthy attention. Looks aren't everything, but the Interest element can certainly do wonders for the personal website. There are so many personal websites out there that are lacking in visual appeal that, by the time someone lands on your website, they will be relieved. There are some simple things and some more complex things you can do to design your website as a point of Interest to your visitors. Keep it simple, whatever "simple" means for your visitor.

## C is Still for Copywriting

Copywriting for your personal website is the task of considering what copy you will write on your web pages. Purposeful Copywriting is the answer to any question about what to write on your web pages, regardless of whether you are blogging or creating a newsletter or making a caption for your picture. Personal website copywriting will follow the same rules mentioned earlier for business websites. You must consider more than just checking spelling and grammar. As always, when making design decisions like writing copy for your website, keep your target audience in mind.

## K is Still for Kickoff

Methods used to market a personal website are similar, and just as plentiful, as the methods used for business websites. When you consider your Kickoff, there are plenty of simple ideas you can work through. Do as much preliminary research as you can prior to spending your entire marketing budget on brochures, business cards, or the like. It is not even necessary to use all of the methods you will learn about in this manual. It is only required that you consider a plan and that your plan include those to whom you will be marketing. It truly makes the most sense, when you think about it. Think of Kickoff as the announcement to the Internet via the world wide web that your personal website is up and running and accessible to all to whom you are targeting. Even if you are re-announcing your presence on the web, you can utilize the Kickoff element to your success.

## Your Website's Prime Real Estate Area

Attention-grabbing website owners realize that the real work is in getting the pertinent information within the website's prime real estate area, the area that fills the web visitor's screen – the area they can see without scrolling further down or further to the right to see it. Seven seconds worth of attention is all you can hope for initially, so making this space count is what you will concentrate on as you design your website. If you have more good stuff to share with the web visitor than you can handle in your website's prime real estate area, use the area to hook your visitor to the really good stuff further within your website.

## Q.U.I.C.K. and Personal

Applying the techniques you have found (and have yet to find) within this manual will help you build your personal website from scratch. There are other, more advanced methods that this manual may suggest that you review with your professional website designer and developer, when you want to take your website to the next level. For now, though, this manual gives you, as a beginner, just enough to quickly get your website up and running if you do not have one.

What if you already have a website? Chances are your website could benefit from at least half of the techniques mentioned within this manual. Remember the Q.U.I.C.K. fix is also for ailing websites – websites that exist but could use some tweaking for various reasons. Reasons for using the Q.U.I.C.K. fix could include a poor website design, a less than desirable flow, an uninteresting website, and so on. The point is that you have decided to take the first step toward fixing your ailing website, or you have decided it is about time you had a personal website of your own. This manual will help you do both – the Q.U.I.C.K. way.

## Q.U.I.C.K. Examples and Applications for a Personal Website

Target audience is an important part of your personal website, because without website visitors, your website is merely a place to park a domain name – not much purpose in that. However, even as important as your audience is in the decision of your purposeful website or any other design or development decision, your purpose really boils down to this question: What do you want your website to accomplish? When you have the answer to that, you will know what type of visitors you need to help you meet your goals.

Useful personal websites cater to your web visitor – just like your business website would. You hope that it is useful enough to a would-be prospect, useful enough to have them consider visiting your website again later or telling some other people about it. Regardless of who your target audience is, a useful and free tool will usually hook your web visitor. However, tools deemed valuable to your website visitor do not have to be free. It really depends on your purpose and your target audience.

Style should be considered very seriously – even with your personal website. There is nothing wrong with adding a little pizzazz to your website, as long as the type of pizzazz you offer is appropriate for your target audience. Even when you do go a little beyond conservative, especially if your audience is a little beyond conservative, the best websites are the most simply-designed websites. It just makes good sense to have your website be easy to navigate with your eyes, even before you touch your mouse to scroll down or over. Your target audience will appreciate you for it, and they will visit again and again.

So if you are a visual artist who is selling her paintings online, and if you intend to attract people who appreciate wild art, the best method for you may be to have your pictures scrolling over a faded leopard skin background. Remember it's okay to get wild with style, but just make it easy for your visitors to navigate and see your pictures with the information to contact you for pricing.

Necessary text is all that is required on your website. Even if your website's Quest is an online newsletter full of discounts for your online book cllub, your text should be exactly relevant to your purpose, and as concise as possible. Make certain that, whatever you do, you recognize the target audience you wish to attract and hold. Remember, you have only about seven seconds to hook your reader – even if your website is clearly a newsletter or a blog. Make sure everything from your title to your picture captions is relevant and concise and driven toward your ultimate goal.

Audience is extremely important in your Kickoff effort. You must get people to your personal website, so you have several decisions to make when planning your online and offline marketing strategy – regardless of whether you operate only online or only offline or a combination of the two. The responsive website traffic you will gain will be well worth the effort.

Good kickoff implementations not only consider the audience, but also consider the ultimate goal. Sure, you already have the best wording possible for your online baseball legend's fan club. Now how will you tell fellow fans how to find you online? Take note of what your target audiences responded to when you reached out to them, then repeat repeat repeat.

## Q.U.I.C.K. Words of Advice…Again

Distracting background techniques do little to attract a would-be buyer, except in very rare circumstances. For example, having music playing in the background will likely only annoy your web visitor, unless you are a musician that must display samples of your music. Another example of annoying techniques is an effect that might make the whole computer screen appear to shake or melt or do some other weird thing – unless you are an independent graphic web artist and have a need to show cool effects and the like. Besides background distractions, websites that serve no purpose are among the biggest Q.U.I.C.K. offenders. While it is true that Quest is just one of the five elements necessary to employ the Q.U.I.C.K. method, it is the most important. Without a purpose for your website, you are misusing your time. More importantly, without the Q, you couldn't spell Q.U.I.C.K.!

# .12.
# Learn Links

## The Missing Link

**Basics.** Traveling between your web pages will be as easy as clicking the hyperlink (link). Otherwise known as links, hyperlinks can be text or images. When you click, you will be

*hyperlink*
*an element in a web page that takes you to another place, usually outside of the web page*

taken to whatever web page is assigned to that link, whether it is another of your web pages or a web page outside of your website. You can even link to another spot within the same web page.

**How to Link Your Web Pages.** In order to have your web pages linked together, you will use <a href= "resources.html">this text will send you to your resource page</a>, for example. Notice the <a href> and </a> tags. This is the basics of linking code. If you have a page about you or your business, a page about a feature product, and your sales order page, as well as your home (index) page, you can link to it by using that code.

**How to Link Within One Page.** To link within one web page, you will need an anchor, which is a marker or placeholder identifying a spot on your page where you want your computer to take someone. The anchor would look like <a href= "#someplace">Move to bottom of page</a>, for example. Your computer would look for a placeholder named "someplace" when your web visitor clicks the Move to bottom of page link. You should note that if you intend to take someone to a specific spot on your web page, there must be enough space beneath it to make up the length of a computer screen. Your code will only take you as far down as your page is long.

## Trixy Wants To Make Some Links

Trixy has an idea for her calendar, and she wants to test linking between pages. Follow along with her to see what she discovers.

**Test a Link Between Web Pages**

1. Open **index-wip.html**, and add the following line anywhere on a separate line between the <body> and </body> tags.

```
<a href="cal.html">My Calendar</a>
```

2. Save and publish.
3. View your domain name followed by /index-wip.html.

**Link a Date to a Description of a Calendar Event**

1. Open **cal.html**.
2. Add the following between the </table> and </body> tags:

```
</br></br></br></br></br></br></br>
</br></br></br></br></br></br></br>
<p><a name="3">Somebody's first anniversary with our company.</a></p>
<p>
</br>
</br>
<a href="#top">Top</a>
</br></br></br></br></br></br></br></br></br>
</br></br></br></br></br></br></br></br></br>
</br></br></br></br></br></br>
```

3. Add the following just above the <table…> tag:

```
<a name="top"></a>
```

4. Replace one of these:

```
<p align="center"> </p>
```

with

```
<p align="center"><a href="#3">Anniversary</a></p>
```

5. Save and publish.
6. View your domain name followed by /index-wip.html and following the link you created to the calendar.

Try moving the link on your work-in-progress home page to somewhere else on the page.

Try making more than one link on the work-in-progress home page.

Try adding a few descriptions on the calendar and making links from your calendar to the matching description.

# .13.
# Create Online Traffic

## Online Traffic Green Light

Websites are useless for bringing attention to your business if you do not have visitors to your website. Regardless of whether you have a business that has a store front or is run out of your home on the computer – if you have a website, you will need traffic. Traffic is related to potential sales. The more website traffic you invite, the more potential buyers will see what you have to offer. The more potential buyers who see what you are selling, the more likely it is that a few of them will buy. It really is simple. It is like fishing – you bait the line, throw the hook in the water, and pull the line in when your hook catches something. You may end up with a fair amount of junk (old sneakers or a locket tossed out to sea), or you may end up with quite a few small fish. But if you stay out there long enough, make yourself available for the catch, you will land the fish of all fishes – eventually.

## On Target for Online

Targeting who will visit your website is important because it increases your chances of a sale. Targeting also utilizes your bandwidth to the maximum advantage, accommodating the people who should be on your website browsing page after page. Your product must be the one that they are looking for, and your service should be, too. If you have done your research ahead of time you know that in order to set yourself apart from other vacuum cleaner sales people, you have to have the newest or best feature ever for the vacuum cleaners you sell. You realize that in order to sell your writing online, you have to pick a specialty that you have experience with that perhaps very few other writers do. So you must do your research into what exactly it is you intend to sell as a product or service for your business to be successful. Your website will foster your effort. Complete with your best-selling product or service, your website will work wonders – once you get the traffic. Then your product or service will get the attention it deserves.

## Count Your Money Later

Visits to your website do not equal money in your bank account – necessarily. It is a long and twisted road, but each web visitor has the potential to be the next sale for you. Here is how it works – sheer numbers. The more web visitors you have, you increase the likelihood that a web visitor will purchase something. Why? Because you already know that, if you have done your offline and online advertising correctly, the people who visit your website are interested in what you have to sell or give them. Factor out a few search engine robots and cyber squatters and possibly competitive websites visiting your website to see what you have to offer, a significant amount of the visits you receive are meant to be there because of something interesting you had to say or show them via marketing efforts – both offline marketing (which we will cover in a later chapter) and online marketing. The greater period of time your website is available via the world wide web, the more your website will filter through the Internet – as long as you make an effort to let the Internet know you are there.

## Strongest Link

**Link Exchange Basics.** Trading website links is a popular, and often misused, online marketing strategy. You could use this to your advantage by understanding both the positive and the less than positive aspects of trading. You have learned in a previous chapter that a link is a direct connection to an existing page on the world wide web. Exchanging links is a reciprocal action. It is where one party agrees to show a link – or a whole text advertisement that links – to another website in exchange for the other website owner doing the same. A primary advantage is that there is a chance that people who visit one website will visit the other websites linked to it. A secondary advantage is that, if you exchange with a complimentary product or service, it can benefit both website owners. A disadvantage is an ad may not be properly shown on a website.

**Think Before You Pay To Link.** There are paid link exchanges and free link exchanges. Just like web host providers, the differences among the paid link exchange providers vary, and so do the

*qualified traffic*
*people who are looking for your products and services*

differences among the free link exchanges. Knowing that, you can imagine that the difference between free and paid link exchanges varies, too. Just be certain to get what you are looking for – traffic. Qualified traffic, people who are looking for your products and services, are a different matter. Some link exchanges make it nice and easy for you by allowing you to include your website in more than one appropriate category listing. Some even let you describe your website in a few sentences, which makes it easier for just the right link exchange partner to find you and vice versa. Search for a **free link exchange**, and make sure you know how it works before you sign up.

**Free to Link.** Business and personal website owners can benefit from using free link exchanges. Exchanging links couldn't be easier. Once you have completed the website you are building (or fixing), you can start getting more traffic to it right away. Use a search engine to search for **free link exchange** and see what you come up with. Keep in mind, that the advertisements that may come up on the right hand side of your screen are usually paid programs, because the advertisers have paid big bucks to advertise in a prime position like that. Also, sometimes when you search you will see the first couple of results are shaded. It is the same scenario where advertisers are hoping to gain your attention anyway they can. If you are looking for free link exchanges, make sure that's what you get.

**Good and Free.** Free link exchanges are full of benefits, the best of which is the cost savings to you. Some of the qualities you can expect to find in the better free link exchanges include: flexibility in your listing, plenty of link exchange topics, ability to reject a link without penalty, many linking members, and easy sign up. While you are trying to decide which link exchange to use, make sure that you have the flexibility to reject links if you want to, because you need to be selective to make certain that you are getting the quality links that you need to increase the chance of attracting quality, and qualified, visitors.

## Permission to Link

**Be Selective.** Visibility across the Internet will be increased exponentially as you stick with reciprocal link exchanges. There are a few basic rules to follow to help you increase the chances of getting your website out there in a positive fashion and save you frustration of deciding on which link exchange partners to include. First, be certain that you are choosing a partner that is not a direct competitor of yours. It may serve you better if you were to include yourself on a website that is complimentary to the product or service that you offer. Second, be certain that you know where your website link will appear. Some website owners make it increasingly difficult for you to find the link exchange partners page, forget about finding your specific text ad. Third, make sure that you are linking to a reputable website, or at least a website with which you wouldn't mind being associated. Read the descriptions carefully – visit the website if you must, at your own risk. To be the best link exchange partner you can be, make sure your website is one that someone would want to associate with, and make sure that the page to your links is prominent enough.

**Missing Links.** Link exchange publishers have rules, one of which is to make sure that if you enter into an agreement to exchange links that you are actually exchanging links. Some link exchange publishers have their own robots (like search engines have their robots) that will search for the links where you have told them they would be when you signed up. Be careful about breaking the rules or you could find yourself banned from a good link exchange program. If a publisher is checking, there will be an area in your account where you can find out about broken link exchange partnerships, and act accordingly.

## Trixy Wants Traffic to Her Website

Trixy is thinking about exchanging links using a free link exchange program. Maybe you could search for one and suggest one to Trixy once she completes her website.

**Option One**

Use a search engine to look for **free link exchange** programs, and choose one or many that meet your standards. Hold onto your list for later.

**Option Two**

Visit www.GetFreeWebsiteTraffic.info for more free online website traffic ideas.

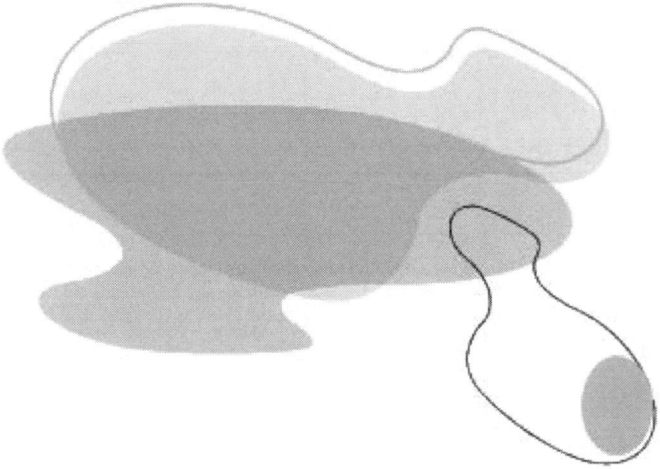

# .14.
# More Style with CSS

## CSS for YOU

Stylizing your web page or your entire website can be as simple as using a Cascading Style Sheet (CSS). Blocks of css code will make your stylization fun an easy. You can use a little or a lot. Include them within a few pages or call up one style sheet for your entire website. It really depends on your layout and other factors as to how you might use CSS, if at all.

**Advanced Styling.** There are some CSS methods that may require a deeper level of understanding than you will acquire here. As with any web design and development, browser type will be a constant pain point. There are methods that professional web designers may be able to use to work around such pain points to make your website look the way you want it to look, regardless of which browser each of your web visitors is using to view your web pages.

## Let's Talk CSS

**Body in CSS.** Background color can be handled with the body {background-color: white;} code. You can also name colors according to the hexadecimal numeral system you learned earlier. For example, {background-color: #FFFFFF;}. You can apply a certain type of font to the whole web page. As long as you didn't specify a font between your <font> and </font> tags, the CSS font would apply by using font-family: arial; for example before the last bracket in the CSS code.

**Fonts in CSS.** There are a few things that you can handle as far as fonts: family, style, and size. You have already learned how you can specify a certain font family (e.g., Times, Arial). As long as your web visitor has in their computer the font which you specify, they should see your web page the way you designed it. As this is not always the case, I would stick with the classic Arial and Times font which most people should have. As for style, there is italic and normal, depending on the font family. Size can range, and you can get varied effects by using the number with or without the px (pixels) versus using the number with a %.

## Use Your CSS When You Want

CSS that you wish to build directly within your web page goes between the header tags of your html page – between <head> and </head>. This is how your computer will know that somewhere on your web page, you want to include your CSS. You build CSS code with a name in front of the code like this: p.maintext{color: red;}. The p means that it affects the paragraph sections <p> tags, and maintext is the name you have assigned. You could have multiple code blocks defining the way the paragraph should look in certain instances – all you have to do is name the instance and call it up when you reach that point in your page. You will get to try this shortly.

## Trixy B. Quick Wants Some Style

Trixy wants to get a resources page up for the link exchange program she found so she can sign up soon to start receiving qualified online traffic. She also wants to add some style to the work-in-progress home page so she can replace the message on her currently unfinished home page. She figures that you might be in the same position, so she has invited you to take the same actions.

**Start a CSS within your cal.html:**

Type the following, per previous instructions, between the <head> and <title> tags:

1. <style type="text/css">
2. p.title{color: lightgreen; font-size: 50px; font-style: italic;}
3. p.maintext{color: red;}
4. body { background-color: lightgreen; font-family: arial;}

5. </style>

Save and view the calendar web page.

Try applying the paragraph CSS parts to your calendar by replacing

<p>

with

<p class="maintext" align="center">1</p>

for example, where the numbered calendar days are.

NOTE: the CSS for the days of the week will not work because you have already defined the color within your html code. If you remove the font color within the html, your CSS will work if you assign it to the days of the week.

Try changing the style of the calendar's title by applying the CSS code:

replace

<p align="center">January</p>

with

<p class="title" align="center">January</p>

Try changing the font for the entire calendar within your CSS code.

Try changing the font colors and sizes within your CSS code.

**Create your Resources page:**

1. Name a blank text editor file as **resources.html**
2. Use the following code as a guide:

```
<html>
<head>
<style type="text/css">
p.title{color: lightgreen; font-size: 50px; font-style: italic;}
p {color: red;}
body { background-color: white; font-family: arial;}
</style>
<title>
This is some title!
</title>
</head>
<body bgcolor="330033">
<p class="title">Resources</p>
<p></p>
<p>Resource #1</p>
<p></p>
<p>Resource #2</p>
<p></p>
<p>Resource #3</p>
</body>
</html>
```

3. Remember to replace the Resources title with whatever title you want this page to have.
4. Save and publish.
5. View your new resources.html page.

# .15.
# Website Copywriting

## Copywriting versus Copyright

Copywriting is the task of considering what text, or copy, to use – in this case you are copywriting for your website. It looks strange to see the word written out, and it almost reads like a typo. However, the definition matches the word – copywriting is writing copy.

A copyright is the rights associated with text, or copy. When you read the first few pages of this manual, before the actual table of contents and chapters, you will notice a copyright statement. This tells you who has the rights to the words as they are assembled in this manual. This means that anyone who duplicates the words as they are written is not only plagiarizing, but also infringing on the copyright holders rights. This act is punishable under law.

## Things to Do

Five guidelines to follow are when copywriting for your web page are:

(1) consider your target audience,

(2) keep your copy brief and to the point,

(3) keep the words as short and simple as possible,

(4) make certain the words are accurate, and

(5) check, double-check, and triple-check for spelling and grammar errors.

Firstly, if you haven't already noticed the glaring theme around your target audience, let me repeat how important that group is to your writing. If you consider who will be reading your website as you write the copy for it, you will save yourself a lot of time. You will also save your readers a lot of frustration.

Secondly, make your writing concise regardless of who your target audience is. Do not keep going on and on trying to make a point. Get to the point right away in making every effort to appeal to the value of your web visitor's time.

Thirdly, keep the words short and simple by avoiding words over three syllables wherever possible.

However, fourthly, make sure that the words you choose accurately describe what you want to say in the context in which you want to say it. Finally, dust off your dictionary and work out all spelling and grammar errors. Use a human editor if necessary.

## Copy Machine

Excessive text is easy to come by on the world wide web. People abuse their web space by putting far too much text on each page, especially the home page, because they are afraid that this will possibly be the only page the web visitor will see. Guess what? If you are thinking like that, and you cram even the most concise and accurate and simply-phrased text onto one area (even if it is a blog), your web visitor will certainly not entertain this one page now or in the future. They already have deemed your website too much to grasp in the time that they have given themselves to search for information, so you will get passed over again and again.

A general rule of thumb is to keep the text on your website to about 250 words, the size of a small article. If you have a newsletter or blog type of website, you may be able to get away with a bit more because of the sheer design of your website, but don't count on it. If you have greater than 250 words (give or take), move on to another page.

## Error-Free and Loving It

**Spelling.** Spelling errors are easy to avoid with a spell checker, right? Consider this:

(1) there are plenty of words that sound alike,

(2) there are plenty more words that are the right word but are used in the wrong context, and

(3) there are still more words that are spelled right – except that those words are not the words you were trying to spell.

The best way to avoid this type of error is to keep your text simple and to the point. Overdoing it by trying to write as others do will frustrate you and will lead to errors. Follow this simple rule to help you write better, then you will have an easier time spell checking your work at the end. Write like you speak. It is that simple. Run the spell checker, but use the good old-fashioned method of reading it a few times. The first review should be at least a day after you have written your work to give it time to settle on the page and give your brain a break from your writing work. Looking at your writing with a fresh set of eyes (especially with someone else's eyes, if you can convince someone else to proofread your work) is the best thing you can do in your effort to avoid spelling errors.

**Grammar.** Grammar errors are about as common as spelling errors. The general rule of thumb is the same as the one rule for avoiding spelling errors – write like you speak. Of course, if you don't know the difference between "they're", "their", and "there", you may need a little more help with spelling and grammar, which you can easily find online by searching the term "common spelling errors" or "common grammar errors". There are plenty of safe and free-to-use websites to help you with the very basics. If you need something more of a remedial English course, perhaps you should look into hiring a freelance writer to handle the writing task for you. There are plenty of resources for this online, including www.LesleyTheWriter.com. Whatever you do, do not get discouraged. Simply recognize when you need help.

## A Few Words on Fonts

**About Face...Font Face.** Attributes for your font are changeable. How you will change them depends on what effect you desire. What affect you desire is, not surprisingly, tied directly to whom you are writing – your target audience. Consider changing your font face, meaning whether your words are curly like the script on a wedding invitation might be or whether your text is more emphasized like the type face on a playbill or a bulletin board announcement or whether your words are styled somewhere in between.

You can change your type face by using the following within the <font face="Arial"> tag. If you are uncertain which name to choose for your type face, open up the word processing software on your computer (e.g., Word) to see what fonts are available. For website pages, it is best to stick with Arial or Times because most people will have these two classic fonts loaded into their computer and will have no problem viewing your text as you intend it to be viewed. If you are using a fancy or new font face that not everyone may have yet, I would suggest consulting with a professional web designer to help you avoid potential viewing problems.

**Font Size.** Enlarging the size of your text is fairly simple in html mode. In your text editor, you would use <span style="font-size:20pt;"> and change the font size to whatever size you desire. An example of where you may want to consider using large text is title text. You may want to decrease your font size for your picture captions.

**Font Color.** Colorizing text is definitely a fun task. Careful attention to surrounding elements is necessary. For example, if you have a light or white background, you should make your text dark so people will not have to strain to see it. Also, if you would like your text to stand out on a solid background, you could consider making your text in a lighter or darker version of that color. For example, if your background is completely red, you may consider cotton candy pink text or maroon text. One thing I would caution against is making your text a complimentary color in relation to your text's background, as it is not only difficult to read but also slightly annoying trying to strain to read the text. For example, red with green and blue with orange.

## Caption Hook

Text should be considered for all areas of your website to hook your reader. Each photo you have should have a descriptive caption, at least a few words. Whether it is a photo of yourself, or a photo of your artwork, or a photo of your latest self-published novel, no picture should be taking up disk space on your website unless it serves a purpose. Even though the saying is that a picture is worth a thousand words, a caption can't hurt.

If you are simply displaying a photo of your fashion design store's opening celebration, caption it appropriately. If you are showing the world wide web what you look like, you could simply put owner or you can put your name, which is far more personable. Regardless of which photos you use, think about what caption you will use as it relates to your purpose on the web and your audience who is looking for exactly what your website has to offer. For instance if you are targeting boot buyers, and you are showing a pair of snake skin boots, caption your picture with the product name so people know what to add to their online shopping cart.

## You Hold the Keywords

Search Engine Optimization (SEO) is big business. There are businesses built on trying to use the power of search engines and how those search engines operate in order to bring traffic to website owners, business and personal. One way you can create your own SEO plan is to make use of keywords. It isn't an exact science, but it is worth a try. Here is why. Even if you are new to using the world wide web, you realize that the fastest way to get the information you need is to use a mega search engine – like Google or Yahoo or Ask – and type in a search term into the search box. What does this mean for you? Try typing in a term to search for a website which might include what your website does. These are the words people are using to try and locate you. The key is to find a word that is broad enough to cover your topic yet specific enough to include a specific area within your topic and then to you. For example, baby deals is too broad and will bring up anything from adoption agencies to deals on baby clothes. However, discount clothes baby will bring up discount clothes – baby clothes to be more specific.

How will you search for your own website in light of what you know now?

## Pro Writer

Copywriting is not for everyone. Fortunately for you, there are plenty of writers out there, many of whom specialize in website copywriting. There is nothing wrong with using an inexpensive website copywriter, but make sure you tell them who you are writing for and what the purpose of your website is. Regardless of which copywriter you choose, it is best to keep this task separate from the website design work that needs to be done. If you choose to use a website designer/developer, make certain that you do not give them the added responsibility of copywriting – unless you are willing to pay extra for it. To do so would be like asking a bakery to make you pancakes – they have all the ingredients to do it, but it is not their specialty, so don't be surprised if they charge you more than a pancake house would charge.

## Help Trixy B. Quick:

Trixy is ready to consider the copy for her website's home page. You could do the same, as you will use it shortly to complete your basic website design project. Take a moment to jot your ideas down on a blank paper offline.

# .16.
# PHP Code

## PHP for YOU

Developing your website can be challenging, but it can also be fun. One way to develop your website and add some usability is to use some of the functions available with php. Introduced in 1995, php is one of those server-side scripts that was mentioned earlier. This manual will show you how to use just enough php code to develop your website enough to capture – and keep – your target audience's attention.

**Advanced PHP.** Versions vary, and it is not likely that you would even want to keep up with all the variations of php out there. Leave the tough stuff to the professionals, and concentrate on the Q.U.I.C.K. php method in this manual. It will be enough to learn the various ways you can use this one script you are about to learn. Since php is a server-side script, it will be viewable across browsers. Whether it will be viewed error-free is really up to how well the code is built. My aim is to keep it simple here, and you will learn how to incorporate a small amount of php code and learn to alter it in a way that suits your purpose. This will add to the functionality of your web pages.

## PHP Talk

**Give Me An Extension.** If you plan to use php code, you must save your web page file with a .php extension. Otherwise, your code will not be viewable. You can place a php code block among html code, but if you don't save the file as .php, you will not see the php.

**Take Me Home.** Your index, or home, page can be php coded. If you use php code, use a .php extension. Unlike any other page, you must make sure that you do not also have an index.html web page file. If you do, you will automatically see that index.html page – even if you have also published an index.php page – when you type your domain name into your browser. The only way you will automatically see the php page when you type your domain name only into the web browser is if you delete your index.html file.

**Tell Your Computer to Code PHP.** The Q.U.I.C.K. way to begin using php is to include it within an html page. When you have located the spot where you want your php to show up, begin your php code as follows: <?php and ending it as ?>.

## PHP Possibilities

Coding in php offers a range of possibilities, all of which focus on a functioning web page – one that gives your web visitors something to do. Php is more web development than web design.

**Save the Date.** Date functions can be used in various ways. The most common is to simply let the user know what day and month and year it is by showing something of a date stamp. That way, when a web visitor sees your website, they will know the time. It is fairly elementary and professional, too.

**Introducing My Date.** Placement of your date code is flexible. For instance, you can include the date code right beneath the title of your newsletter website. You could include the date code directly above the relevant links section located in the middle of your blog website. The possibilities are only limited by your imagination. Remember your prime website real estate? Consider whether or not to put your date code within that area for an added convenience.

## Trixy Wants the Current Date on Her Calendar Page

Trixy likes what she is learning about development, and she wants to add the current date to her calendar. Perhaps you would like to do the same.

Open cal.html and save as **cal.php**, so that your computer knows you want to use a php code.

Replace

```
<p align="center"> </p>
```

with

```
<p align="center"><?php
echo date("m/d/y");
?></p>
```

If you are using Host Likely, then you can make a new file called **cal.php** from your public_html folder. Save the original calendar code to the php file, and make the replacement as described.

Try assigning the maintext CSS code to the paragraph's main text, where the date code is.

Try changing the color of the CSS code block for the paragraph's main text.

Use a different date format:

replace

```
"m/d/y"
```

with

```
"D, M. Y"
```

Use a long date instead:

replace

"D, M. Y"

with

"l, F j, Y"

Try moving your date to another location on your page.

# .17.
# Get Offline Traffic

## Please Repeat That

Marketing efforts to increase traffic to your website from sources outside of the Internet should be considered carefully. Depending on your <u>time budget</u>, and to a larger degree your <u>monetary budget</u>,

*time budget*
*the time you allocate to something*

*monetary budget*
*the money you allocate to something*

you may spend as little as one hour a day or as much as three hours. There really is no magic formula. Advertising works through repetition, so you must have multiple repetitions of your message in front of as many qualified people as possible. Of your target audience, about two percent are going to give your information a second glance. Of those two percent, only half will buy – maybe. So plan a strategy that you can afford – time-wise and money-wise – to repeat again and again.

## Nothing Is Too Little…So Do More Than Nothing

*marketing*
*the consideration of product, pricing, distribution, and promotional efforts of a product or service; includes sales strategy*

Quality of offline marketing strategies matters more than quantity. Realize that you must market in some way. Do not make the mistake of thinking that search engines and people will find your website just because you have published it. Use techniques – as many as you have time or money for – to get traffic to your business website.

## Your Finest Deck of Cards

**Business Cards.** Information contained on a business card is the essential contact information. Usually it includes your name, and an indication of what you do as a business person. Since you are this far in the manual, you realize that you must also include your website address on the business card. Typically a phone number is included as well, because we realize that not everyone is inclined to visit your website in order to get your other contact information. The business card immediately leaves an image of a person who is serious about his or her business. Even if you have more of a personal following, like an author would or a poet, a business card lets people know that it is more than just a hobby for you.

Business cards are best used at business card exchanges and events that require you to represent your business in a more professional light. Certainly you can include a business card with a business proposal to a bank or another financier to help get your business off the ground, or money to further establish your presence in the community, or even obtain grant money from government or other agencies.

**Promotion Cards.** Promotion cards usually are more centered around a specific event and do not typically include your name. These are more like the cards you may see stuck beneath your windshield, which you would certainly not want to do yourself as a professional person. However, you can also use them in other more appropriate ways. Promotion cards are better suited for more casual events, as an after-work social gathering among friends or other business professionals in a more casual setting. Use your promotional card, complete with your website address, at community affairs like festivals or even conventions that are more in line with personal activities – craft fairs, computer shows, etc. Remember, you are using this type of card to promote an event.

**Passing Out Is the New Way to Make Money.** Website traffic will not flow just because you have your web address on your business card or promotion card. It is now time to get that card out there, make the moves to get those cards in as many eager hands as possible. Go to as many events – business or social – as possible, and as appropriate. For example if you are a business, you are able to go to social events – just choose your events carefully to be certain you have a chance of being around people who want or need your service and who will take you seriously even having met you at a social affair. If you have a personal website, you can still go to business affairs as appropriate if it will put you in front of the correct audience of people who may benefit from whatever event you are promoting. Who knows? You may be able to find sponsors in some cases.

## Share Your News with Us

**Newsletter Basics.** News about your industry or profession or area of expertise is a great way to get people interested in what you have to offer as a business. Information is free for the newsletter recipient and is a relatively low cost to produce, considering the high returns it could bring the newsletter publisher. If you are going to use this method to drive traffic to your website, make sure you develop a newsletter with your target in mind. What readership level does your web visitor most likely have? What are the types of information that would interest your target? How is your audience's attention span? For example, if you are targeting children (and their parents) for your service online, you may want to consider splitting your newsletter into a parent's section and a child's section, if the children are at reading level. This will likely be a very short and light-on-news newsletter. You may consider something more of a tale which continues so they will look forward to the tale in the next newsletter. Better yet, tell them that they can follow the tale online at your website. Whatever you do, tell your audience about your website and pick a newsletter topic that surrounds your business but is not directly about your business. It needs to present a real or perceived issue that your company can solve.

**Place News Here.** Placement of your newsletter depends on where your audience is. Continuing with the business that sells a children's product, ask yourself: Where do parents (the senior decision makers) go with their children (the junior decision makers)? You may consider explaining to the local children's dentist the purpose of your free newsletter to see if they may let you place a few copies in their waiting room. You could probably think of a few more examples immediately, but remember that it must reach the parent (the ultimate decision maker) while he or she is likely to be with the child (the one who mommy and daddy can't say "no" to) in order to be the most effective. If you have a less complex target audience structure, it should be even easier for you to imagine where you could put your newsletter.

## Around Your Community

Free community bulletin boards are an excellent way to get word of your website around a particular community. Colorful strips of paper in various sizes adorn these community bulletin boards making a jumbled mess of things sometimes, but if you get the right information in front of the right people, it could be worth the amount of time you spend applying this method. Make sure you are in the correct community.

For example, if you have a service for college students, don't bother placing your ad in grocery stores – not even the one just outside the school campus. That would be misusing your time budget. Advertise directly on campus bulletin boards instead. You're probably thinking "students go grocery shopping, too" and you're right. However, if you value your time, just get to where the target is most likely to be during the normal course of their day.

Communities are all about sharing information, but you may have to actually join the community. Just make sure you have permission, whether you are part of the community or not. Find out who's in charge of the community board. For some places, like the bookstore, it is as simple as asking to use their bulletin board. For other places, like a college campus, you may have to visit student services.

## Sign Your Car Over

Advertisement can be carried out creatively. You've seen the cars with the beauty representative stickers on them. These business people are using their car or truck or whatever as a multi-purpose vehicle. There is no reason why you can't do the same. Keep in mind who your target audience is and where they are likely to be while you are driving around with a sign on your car. Suppose you are trying to target stay-at-home moms. If you work full-time in another position where you will not be driving your own car during the day when these mothers may be out – grocery shopping or shopping for their children or taking their children to the park for some air – then you are misusing your monetary budget with this form of advertising.

## Your Newest Lawn Ornament

Information dissemination to these stay-at-home moms who travel with their children is still possible. Techniques such as using a lawn sign may be perfect for you, in this case. If you realize that you live in a neighborhood full of stay-at-home moms, you could design (or have someone else design) a short, nifty, easy-to-read sign on paper and take it to your local sign shop. In a couple of days, you could have your advertisement up...if you have your own lawn. If you rent your home or live in a rental apartment, you may not be permitted to advertise in this manner. Also, if you are worried about the tax consequences of doing business at home, seek out a tax professional's help before using this method.

## Business with Web Benefits

Techniques are available for "forcing" your target audience to visit your website. This is especially important if your target audience is not familiar with using the Internet. Let them in on the benefits of checking out your business online. Remember that example earlier of the business person who has a children's product? Suppose you were that business owner and you decided to have a running tale to entertain the junior decision maker – a tale that can also be found online. What if your product was supplemental to the tale? For example, if the tale were about dragons who didn't care for their teeth, and you sold one-of-a-kind toothbrushes, the influential junior decision maker would find the tale engaging and the real decision maker would find it relevant. They would visit your website to read more about the tale and to buy your exclusive, one-of-a-kind tooth brush. Better yet, you still followed the suggested rules from earlier in this chapter: to have your newsletter be relevant and not just a sales pitch for your product.

## Online, Offline, No Fine Line

**Take the Combo Meal.** Variations and combinations of the offline methods suggested in this manual are possible. You have choices: (a) use none, (b) use only online methods, (c) use only offline methods, or (d) use some combination of online and offline methods. Just remember that your goal is to get traffic to your website, and as much of it as possible. It is equally as important to consider your monetary and time budgets.

Just as if you were to do a direct mail campaign for your offline business, you would hopefully select a large list of people to mail to who could use or who need your product. For example, if you were to do a direct mail campaign for a flower shop, you may mail to a list of all the single, eligible males in Newark, Delaware, based on whatever you tell yourself "eligible" is. Suppose there are 100,000 such males. Of those 100,000, only 2% are likely to even be interested enough to pause before throwing the mailer away. Of that 2,000, only half are likely to back away from the trashcan and set it aside to read more later. Of that 1,000, only about half are likely to actually call or visit your website.

You must realize that the more variations – and the more repetitions of whatever you choose to do – the more website traffic you will receive as a result. Different methods of advertising will appeal to different people.

## Trixy Builds Her Offline Strategy for Gaining Online Traffic

Trixy knows the value of an offline marketing strategy to get website traffic, and she has narrowed down her options to the following two sources that she wants to share with you. The two options below can help her with any of the offline strategies mentioned in this chapter, and more.

**Option One**

Explore the options available at Copy & Mail Xpress.

**Option Two**

Explore the options available at www.TrueMM.com.

# .18.
# JavaScript Code

## JavaScript...No Sugar, Please

JavaScript is another type of script to aid in the development of web pages. It can liven up your web page like coffee might liven up some people. However, JavaScript is not the same as Java. What you really need to understand is that, because it is a client-side script (mentioned earlier in this manual), not all web browsers will accept it. Really, a user may have to choose to accept to view JavaScript enabled web pages. In order to understand how to let others know how to enable

JavaScript to view your web page, check to see if you have JavaScript enabled.

**JavaScript Enabling.** Look at the menu bar on your web browser. Click the Tools menu. If you are using FireFox 3.0, choose Options... and you will immediately see a few options that will be checked (meaning you want to be able to use that feature) or unchecked (meaning you do not want that feature to be available to you). Make sure there is a check in the box beside Enable JavaScript, and click OK. If you are using Internet Explorer 6.0, choose Internet Options, Security, Custom Level..., and scroll down to Scripting. Under the Active Scripting section, click Enable, then OK. There may be slight variations depending on your browser version.

## Addicted to JavaScript

**Getting Started.** JavaScript offers several options for developing your website. Work with your professional web developer to determine which of the more advanced methods may – or may not be – necessary for the proper development of your website. Here, I will give you a fairly simple method of using JavaScript to enhance the functionality of your web page. Start by letting your computer know that you will include JavaScript in your web page. Place this <style type="text/javascript"></style> between your <head> and <title> tags within your web page. Look familiar? If you remember this from the CSS chapter, you have a good memory. Note that you cannot define more than one style per web page. Professional website developers can, but as far as this self-paced course goes, you will run into a problem. What this means is that you will use regular html specifications for your fonts instead of CSS when you are coding a particular web page JavaScript.

**Change of Scenery.** You are going to learn how to allow your web visitor to change the background color of your web page. This could be especially useful and fun. You can imagine the applications later. But now, think about your favorite colors and get ready as you and Trixy get dangerously close to completing your respective websites. Previously, you learned how php can be combined with hyperlinks and a table in the form of a calendar. The code you are about to learn combines JavaScript with hyperlinks and tables. It is flexible enough to put anywhere on your web page. Though the code is rather long, especially once you combine it with the copy you will write for your web page, the result for this JavaScript code is truly just as long as whatever word you are using for the text effect. Trixy is waiting patiently for you to get finished reading so the both of you can try coding a change of background color.

## Trixy Wants to Complete Her Website

Trixy has finished writing copy for her main web page on loose leaf paper. She has set it aside to consider the final look of her new website. After reading about JavaScript, she decides it is time to pull it all together and finalize her home page, her calendar page, and her resources page for a well-made three-page website.

**The Main Copy for the Home Page**

Open your **index-wip.html** page, and replace the entire contents with the following code (or you can email Lesley the Web Resource for the complete website code: email@lesleythewebresource.com.):

```
<html>
<head>
```

```
<style type="text/javascript"></style>
<title>
Welcome!
</title>
</head>
<body bgcolor="#330033" leftmargin="0" marginwidth="0" topmargin="0" marginheight="0">
<table bgcolor="white" width="630" height="293" align="center" cellpadding="0" cellspacing="0" style="margin-top:0; margin-bottom:0;">
<tr>
<td width="630" colspan="4">
<p style="margin-top:0; margin-bottom:0;" align="center"><span style="font-size:36pt;"><font face="Arial" color="#330033">Web Page Introduction Title</font></span></p>
</td>
</tr>
<tr style="margin-top:0; margin-bottom:0;">
<td width="210" style="margin-top:0; margin-bottom:0;">
<p style="margin-top:0; margin-right:5; margin-bottom:0; margin-left:5;" align="left"><font face="Arial"><span style="margin-top:0; margin-right:5; margin-bottom:0; margin-left:5;"><a href="index.html">Home</a> | <a href="cal.html">Events</a> | <a href="resources.html">Resources</a></span></font></p>
</td>
<td width="51" style="margin-top:0; margin-bottom:0;"> </td>
<td width="369" style="margin-top:0; margin-bottom:0;" colspan="2"> </td>
</tr>
<tr>
<td width="210">
<p style="margin-top:0; margin-right:5; margin-bottom:0; margin-left:5;" align="left"><font face="Arial"><span style="font-size:12pt;"><img src="images/hosting.png" width="200" border="0"></span></font></p>
<p style="margin-top:0; margin-right:5; margin-bottom:0; margin-left:5;" align="center"><font face="Arial"><span style="font-size:8pt;">Some Image Caption</span></font></p>
</td>
```

```
<td width="420" colspan="3">
<p style="margin-top:0; margin-right:5; margin-bottom:0; margin-left:5;" align="left"><font face="Arial"><span style="font-size:12pt;"> </span></font></p>
<p style="margin-top:0; margin-right:5; margin-bottom:0; margin-left:5;" align="left"><font face="Arial"><span style="font-size:12pt;">This is the part you've been waiting for.  This is your main website page.  Of course, you will have to do all of the work of writing copy for your web page.  You've made it this far.  Now, there is not much left to do.  If you have worked through the examples with Trixy, you should be viewing this page as a work in progress.  </span></font></p>
<p style="margin-top:0; margin-right:5; margin-bottom:0; margin-left:5;" align="left"> </p>
<p style="margin-top:0; margin-right:5; margin-bottom:0; margin-left:5;" align="left"><font face="Arial"><span style="font-size:12pt;">You will have to adjust the text depending on how many words you are using.  And remember to consider all of the Q.U.I.C.K. elements.</span></font></p>
<p style="margin-top:0; margin-right:5; margin-bottom:0; margin-left:5;" align="left"> </p>
<p style="margin-top:0; margin-right:5; margin-bottom:0; margin-left:5;" align="left"><font face="Arial"><span style="font-size:12pt;">You have options.  I cannot begin to tell you which picture to choose, or if to choose one at all.  Nor can I tell you to have a calendar or date on your website.  It is completely up to you</span></font><span style="margin-top:0; margin-bottom:0;">.</span></p>
</td>
</tr>
<tr>
<td width="210">
<p style="margin-top:0; margin-right:5; margin-bottom:0; margin-left:5;" align="center"><font face="Arial"><span style="font-size:12pt;">Any favorite colors?</span></font></p>
<p style="margin-top:0; margin-right:5; margin-bottom:0; margin-left:5;" align="center"><A HREF="" onMouseOver="document.bgColor='white'">white</a></br>
<A HREF="" onMouseOver="document.bgColor='tan'">tan</a></br>
<A HREF="" onMouseOver="document.bgColor='#330033'">deep
```

```
purple</a></br>
<A HREF="" onMouseOver="document.bgColor='lightgreen'">light green</a></br>
<A HREF="" onMouseOver="document.bgColor='lightblue'">light blue</a></br>
<A HREF="" onMouseOver="document.bgColor='orange'">orange</a>
</p>
</td>
<td width="200" colspan="2">
<p style="margin-top:0; margin-right:5; margin-bottom:0; margin-left:5;" align="left"> </p>
<p style="margin-top:0; margin-right:5; margin-bottom:0; margin-left:5;" align="left"><font face="Arial"><span style="font-size:12pt;">You will make sure that you have followed the suggestions in the copywriting chapter of the Q.U.I.C.K. Fix for Your Ailing (or Missing) Website.</span></font></p>
</td>
<td width="220">
<div align="left">
<table border="1" width="208" style="margin-top:0; margin-right:5; margin-bottom:0; margin-left:5;">
<tr>
<td width="198" colspan="7">
<p align="center" style="margin-top:0; margin-right:5; margin-bottom:0; margin-left:5;"><span style="font-size:12pt;"><b><font face="Arial" color="#CC0000"><a href="cal.html">January</a></font></b></span></p>
</td>
</tr>
<tr>
<td width="23" bgcolor="#990000">
<p style="margin-top:0; margin-right:5; margin-bottom:0; margin-left:5;" align="left"><font face="Arial"><span style="font-size:8pt;"><b>U</b></span></font><font face="Arial"><span style="font-size:12pt;"></span></font></p>
</td>
<td width="23" bgcolor="#990000">
<p style="margin-top:0; margin-right:5; margin-bottom:0; margin-left:5;"
```

```
align="left"><font face="Arial"><span style="font-size:8pt;"><b>M</b></span></font><font face="Arial"><span style="font-size:12pt;"></span></font></p>
</td>
<td width="23" bgcolor="#990000">
<p style="margin-top:0; margin-right:5; margin-bottom:0; margin-left:5;" align="left"><font face="Arial"><span style="font-size:8pt;"><b>T</b></span></font><font face="Arial"><span style="font-size:12pt;"></span></font></p>
</td>
<td width="23" bgcolor="#990000">
<p style="margin-top:0; margin-right:5; margin-bottom:0; margin-left:5;" align="left"><font face="Arial"><span style="font-size:8pt;"><b>W</b></span></font><font face="Arial"><span style="font-size:12pt;"></span></font></p>
</td>
<td width="23" bgcolor="#990000">
<p style="margin-top:0; margin-right:5; margin-bottom:0; margin-left:5;" align="left"><font face="Arial"><span style="font-size:8pt;"><b>R</b></span></font><font face="Arial"><span style="font-size:12pt;"></span></font></p>
</td>
<td width="23" bgcolor="#990000">
<p style="margin-top:0; margin-right:5; margin-bottom:0; margin-left:5;" align="left"><font face="Arial"><span style="font-size:8pt;"><b>F</b></span></font><font face="Arial"><span style="font-size:12pt;"></span></font></p>
</td>
<td width="23" bgcolor="#990000">
<p style="margin-top:0; margin-right:5; margin-bottom:0; margin-left:5;" align="left"><font face="Arial"><span style="font-size:8pt;"><b>S</b></span></font><font face="Arial"><span style="font-size:12pt;"></span></font></p>
</td>
</tr>
<tr>
<td width="23">
```

```
<p style="margin-top:0; margin-right:5; margin-bottom:0; margin-left:5;" align="left"><font face="Arial"><span style="font-size:8pt;"> </span></font></p>
</td>
<td width="23" bgcolor="#FFFF99">
<p style="margin-top:0; margin-right:5; margin-bottom:0; margin-left:5;" align="left"><font face="Arial"><span style="font-size:8pt;">1</span></font><font face="Arial"><span style="font-size:12pt;"></span></font></p>
</td>
<td width="23" bgcolor="#FFFF99">
<p style="margin-top:0; margin-right:5; margin-bottom:0; margin-left:5;" align="left"><font face="Arial"><span style="font-size:8pt;">2</span></font><font face="Arial"><span style="font-size:12pt;"></span></font></p>
</td>
<td width="23" bgcolor="#FFFF99">
<p style="margin-top:0; margin-right:5; margin-bottom:0; margin-left:5;" align="left"><font face="Arial"><span style="font-size:8pt;">3</span></font><font face="Arial"><span style="font-size:12pt;"></span></font></p>
</td>
<td width="23" bgcolor="#FFFF99">
<p style="margin-top:0; margin-right:5; margin-bottom:0; margin-left:5;" align="left"><font face="Arial"><span style="font-size:8pt;">4</span></font><font face="Arial"><span style="font-size:12pt;"></span></font></p>
</td>
<td width="23" bgcolor="#FFFF99">
<p style="margin-top:0; margin-right:5; margin-bottom:0; margin-left:5;" align="left"><font face="Arial"><span style="font-size:8pt;">5</span></font><font face="Arial"><span style="font-size:12pt;"></span></font></p>
</td>
<td width="23">
<p style="margin-top:0; margin-right:5; margin-bottom:0; margin-left:5;" align="left"><font face="Arial"><span style="font-
```

```
size:8pt;">6</span></font><font face="Arial"><span style="font-
size:12pt;"></span></font></p>
</td>
</tr>
<tr>
<td width="23">
<p style="margin-top:0; margin-right:5; margin-bottom:0; margin-left:5;"
align="left"><font face="Arial"><span style="font-
size:8pt;">7</span></font><font face="Arial"><span style="font-
size:12pt;"></span></font></p>
</td>
<td width="23" bgcolor="#FFFF99">
<p style="margin-top:0; margin-right:5; margin-bottom:0; margin-left:5;"
align="left"><font face="Arial"><span style="font-
size:8pt;">8</span></font><font face="Arial"><span style="font-
size:12pt;"></span></font></p>
</td>
<td width="23" bgcolor="#FFFF99">
<p style="margin-top:0; margin-right:5; margin-bottom:0; margin-left:5;"
align="left"><font face="Arial"><span style="font-
size:8pt;">9</span></font><font face="Arial"><span style="font-
size:12pt;"></span></font></p>
</td>
<td width="23" bgcolor="#FFFF99">
<p style="margin-top:0; margin-right:5; margin-bottom:0; margin-left:5;"
align="left"><font face="Arial"><span style="font-
size:8pt;">10</span></font><font face="Arial"><span style="font-
size:12pt;"></span></font></p>
</td>
<td width="23" bgcolor="#FFFF99">
<p style="margin-top:0; margin-right:5; margin-bottom:0; margin-left:5;"
align="left"><font face="Arial"><span style="font-
size:8pt;">11</span></font><font face="Arial"><span style="font-
size:12pt;"></span></font></p>
</td>
<td width="23" bgcolor="#FFFF99">
<p style="margin-top:0; margin-right:5; margin-bottom:0; margin-left:5;"
```

```
align="left"><font face="Arial"><span style="font-size:8pt;">12</span></font><font face="Arial"><span style="font-size:12pt;"></span></font></p>
</td>
<td width="23">
<p style="margin-top:0; margin-right:5; margin-bottom:0; margin-left:5;" align="left"><font face="Arial"><span style="font-size:8pt;">13</span></font><font face="Arial"><span style="font-size:12pt;"></span></font></p>
</td>
</tr>
<tr>
<td width="23">
<p style="margin-top:0; margin-right:5; margin-bottom:0; margin-left:5;" align="left"><font face="Arial"><span style="font-size:8pt;">14</span></font><font face="Arial"><span style="font-size:12pt;"></span></font></p>
</td>
<td width="23" bgcolor="#FFFF99">
<p style="margin-top:0; margin-right:5; margin-bottom:0; margin-left:5;" align="left"><font face="Arial"><span style="font-size:8pt;">15</span></font><font face="Arial"><span style="font-size:12pt;"></span></font></p>
</td>
<td width="23" bgcolor="#FFFF99">
<p style="margin-top:0; margin-right:5; margin-bottom:0; margin-left:5;" align="left"><font face="Arial"><span style="font-size:8pt;">16</span></font><font face="Arial"><span style="font-size:12pt;"></span></font></p>
</td>
<td width="23" bgcolor="#FFFF99">
<p style="margin-top:0; margin-right:5; margin-bottom:0; margin-left:5;" align="left"><font face="Arial"><span style="font-size:8pt;">17</span></font><font face="Arial"><span style="font-size:12pt;"></span></font></p>
</td>
<td width="23" bgcolor="#FFFF99">
```

```
<p style="margin-top:0; margin-right:5; margin-bottom:0; margin-left:5;" align="left"><font face="Arial"><span style="font-size:8pt;">18</span></font><font face="Arial"><span style="font-size:12pt;"></span></font></p>
</td>
<td width="23" bgcolor="#FFFF99">
<p style="margin-top:0; margin-right:5; margin-bottom:0; margin-left:5;" align="left"><font face="Arial"><span style="font-size:8pt;">19</span></font><font face="Arial"><span style="font-size:12pt;"></span></font></p>
</td>
<td width="23">
<p style="margin-top:0; margin-right:5; margin-bottom:0; margin-left:5;" align="left"><font face="Arial"><span style="font-size:8pt;">20</span></font><font face="Arial"><span style="font-size:12pt;"></span></font></p>
</td>
</tr>
<tr>
<td width="23">
<p style="margin-top:0; margin-right:5; margin-bottom:0; margin-left:5;" align="left"><font face="Arial"><span style="font-size:8pt;">21</span></font></p>
</td>
<td width="23" bgcolor="#FFFF99">
<p style="margin-top:0; margin-right:5; margin-bottom:0; margin-left:5;" align="left"><font face="Arial"><span style="font-size:8pt;">22</span></font></p>
</td>
<td width="23" bgcolor="#FFFF99">
<p style="margin-top:0; margin-right:5; margin-bottom:0; margin-left:5;" align="left"><font face="Arial"><span style="font-size:8pt;">23</span></font></p>
</td>
<td width="23" bgcolor="#FFFF99">
<p style="margin-top:0; margin-right:5; margin-bottom:0; margin-left:5;" align="left"><font face="Arial"><span style="font-
```

```
size:8pt;">24</span></font></p>
</td>
<td width="23" bgcolor="#FFFF99">
<p style="margin-top:0; margin-right:5; margin-bottom:0; margin-left:5;" align="left"><font face="Arial"><span style="font-size:8pt;">25</span></font></p>
</td>
<td width="23" bgcolor="#FFFF99">
<p style="margin-top:0; margin-right:5; margin-bottom:0; margin-left:5;" align="left"><font face="Arial"><span style="font-size:8pt;">26</span></font></p>
</td>
<td width="23">
<p style="margin-top:0; margin-right:5; margin-bottom:0; margin-left:5;" align="left"><font face="Arial"><span style="font-size:8pt;">27</span></font></p>
</td>
</tr>
<tr>
<td width="23">
<p style="margin-top:0; margin-right:5; margin-bottom:0; margin-left:5;" align="left"><font face="Arial"><span style="font-size:8pt;">28</span></font></p>
</td>
<td width="23" bgcolor="#FFFF99">
<p style="margin-top:0; margin-right:5; margin-bottom:0; margin-left:5;" align="left"><font face="Arial"><span style="font-size:8pt;">29</span></font></p>
</td>
<td width="23" bgcolor="#FFFF99">
<p style="margin-top:0; margin-right:5; margin-bottom:0; margin-left:5;" align="left"><font face="Arial"><span style="font-size:8pt;">30</span></font></p>
</td>
<td width="23" bgcolor="#FFFF99">
<p style="margin-top:0; margin-right:5; margin-bottom:0; margin-left:5;" align="left"><font face="Arial"><span style="font-
```

```
size:8pt;">31</span></font></p>
</td>
<td width="23">
<p style="margin-top:0; margin-right:5; margin-bottom:0; margin-left:5;" align="left"><font face="Arial"><span style="font-size:8pt;"> </span></font></p>
</td>
<td width="23">
<p style="margin-top:0; margin-right:5; margin-bottom:0; margin-left:5;" align="left"><font face="Arial"><span style="font-size:8pt;"> </span></font></p>
</td>
<td width="23">
<p style="margin-top:0; margin-right:5; margin-bottom:0; margin-left:5;" align="left"><font face="Arial"><span style="font-size:8pt;"> </span></font></p>
</td>
</tr>
</table>
</div>
</td>
</tr>
<tr>
<td width="630" height="29" colspan="4">
<p style="margin-top:0; margin-right:5; margin-bottom:0; margin-left:5;" align="left"><font face="Arial"><span style="font-size:12pt;"> </span></font></p>
<p style="margin-top:0; margin-right:5; margin-bottom:0; margin-left:5;" align="left"><font face="Arial"><span style="font-size:12pt;">Once you have a good understanding of how to build a basic web page, you are ready to share it.  If you need to, review the manual again.  Remember, it is self-paced.  There is no pressure.  Just make it a good website.  One that is Q.U.I.C.K.  By the way, this web page contains 250 words, including the heading title, caption, links, and
date.  If you want a more advanced website,
you know where to find me...and Trixy!</span></font></p>
<p style="margin-top:0; margin-bottom:0;"> </p>
```

```
</td>
</tr>
</table>
</body>
</html>
```

**Did you remember to replace your image with one you have saved in your web page files?**

**Publish and View to Make Sure It Works.**

Visit your domain name followed by **/index-wip.html**, and note that the link to the home page will be the home page that is currently published – it should still be a blank page with your title in the menu bar, unless you have changed it.

**Add the Copy You Wrote, and Adjust As Necessary.**

**Publish to View It.**

**Add a Current Date.**
Save index-wip.html as **index-wip.php**.

NOTE: If you are using Host Likely web hosting service, select index-wip.html from the public_html file folders and rename file as index-wip.php from the menu that appears on the right side.

Replace

```
<td width="369" style="margin-top:0; margin-bottom:0;"
colspan="2"> </td>
```

with

```
<td width="369" style="margin-top:0; margin-bottom:0;" colspan="2">Today
is <?php echo date("l, F j, Y"); ?></td>
```

Save and publish.

View your domain name followed by **index-wip.php**.

**Review and Publish Your Website.**

If everything looks good on the work-in-progress page, save that page as **index.php** and remove the index.html file from your public_html folder.

If you did everything correctly, you should see your website once you type your domain name in the browser. It should have your web copy and your code to change the background color and a current date stamp, as well as a calendar in the middle of the page. All of your links should work.

If anything is missing or not working, please review the manual.

Try adding the same set of links to your Resources and Calendar pages.

Sign up for the online link exchange program you like, using your resources.html page as the linking page.

Try various color combinations throughout your website.

Try changing the color choices in the background color selector.

Try updating your calendar to the proper month, and add the year.

Try reviewing the manual to see what else you can update.

# .19.
# Secure Your Website

## I'm Calling Security

If you have your web visitors send you information via your website, then security for your website is an absolute must. Two types of security are required: your security and the security of your web visitors. We will define exactly what each type of security consideration is and what you can do about it for your website.

A Secure Socket Layer (SSL) certificate, or digital certificate, is important for encrypting information being passed through your website from your visitors. It also verifies you as the legitimate owner of the domain name to give your web visitors peace of mind. Domain-Name validation – SSL certificates that only verify that you own the domain name – is an inexpensive option which still provides the same important ability to scramble the information being sent over your website from would-be web criminals, so that only you, the intended party, will see the message as it is intended once it reaches your email box. You can purchase one usually through your web host provider.

Another type of security, which SSL does not cover, is virus protection from nasty worms and bots you may receive while using free software, or while receiving unknown (sometimes known) email which is infected. Be sure to consider getting your computer swept for viruses by a reputable and reliable company as soon as possible in order for your computer to function at its optimal level.

## Uh, We Don't Cover That

Security of information is one of the two main purposes of an SSL. That assurance is mainly for your web visitors so that they know they are passing information as securely as possible over the Internet. It will not protect against viruses, it will not protect information on your desktop from being viewed if an outside program puts spyware on your computer, it will not provide a password for your web page. SSL is solely for the purpose of protecting information passed over the Internet, and it validates that you have the right to protect the web page you are protecting – it identifies you to the world wide web.

## Security Check versus Paycheck

SSL costs will vary from supplier to supplier. It is more important to realize whether or not you truly need one and which type to use before getting discouraged by the price tag. Another consideration would be whether or not you can afford to go without this type of protection – consider what your cost would be (e.g., loss of customer trust, or never gaining enough trust). SSL certificate comparison is usually not apples-to-apples, as different providers offer more or less of one feature or another, or the type of security is not the same as one or another provider.

## Vision of Security

**Browser.** Visual representation of security is easily apparent with a padlock. Think of a padlock you would use at a storage facility. It is a universal symbol of security and protection for valuable items. So it is with your website. As well, the https:// in your browser represents the secure version of an http:// website. As long as the path to your images is directed to the secured version of your web pages, your users will enjoy a secure existence on your website. They will be confident that you are who you say you are, or at least that you own the domain name that is on your business card or marketing material, and they will be able to shop or send you information or whatever you want within a secure environment.

*http*
*hyper text transfer protocol; defines how messages are formatted and transmitted*

*https*
*secure transmission of single web pages*

*path*
*list of directories to a particular file location*

**Errors.** Errors related to your website's security certificate can deter would be clients. In order to avoid the yellow caution sign errors, examine the three areas of information related to your SSL certificate:

(a) what domain name the certificate is for

(b) who the certificate is issued by

(c) a date range, which represents the date the certificate was issued and the date it expires.

If your web visitor were to click on the padlock, they will see green check marks beside the three areas named above, followed by the respective bits of information. If there is a yellow caution icon in any of the three areas, the problem is related to the respective area. For example, if you have a security certificate for yourdomain.com, but you had it installed on mydomain.com, an error would appear. If your certificate were installed improperly (e.g., if you had no chain of trust or some higher authority validating that you own the domain name, for example), an error would appear. If today was one day past January 10$^{th}$, 2000 when your certificate expired, an error would appear.

**Site Seal Logo.** Visual security representation does not end with the https:// or the padlock. There is another immediate way of acknowledging your website as a secure website – the site seal or secure logo seal. You should check with your SSL certificate provider – whether it is your web host provider or an outside service provider – for details on cost and installation. It is well worth the perceived value your web visitor will place on your website above your competitor's poorly secured site – especially if your web visitor has to submit even one bit of personal information to receive the benefit of your services.

# .20.
# Lesley the Web Resource, LLC

## Website Hosting Service

Let us host your website so that you may bring your perfect website to the Internet via the world wide web. Host Likely website hosting service is the perfect place for the website you have just fixed or created with this Q.U.I.C.K. Fix self-paced manual. Learn more about the hosting club benefits by visiting www.LesleyTheWebResource.com today.

## DIY Website Design and Development

At one point, you may have already taken the initiative to design your own web page. You are obviously still interested in taking matters into your own hands, or you would not have gotten this self-paced manual. If this is your first attempt at building your own website, then you have invested well. Lesley the Web Resource, LLC is the source for do-it-yourself web design and development. On the most basic level, we provide helpful tips and scripts through various online and offline resources. This self-paced manual is a good start. However, if you would like more, you should check out www.LesleyTheWebResource.com directly and click on the DIY links to get you the basic web design you are seeking.

## Custom Website Design and Development

Naturally, Lesley the Web Resource, LLC still designs and develops websites. If you like what you have learned in this book, then let us take your website design and development to the next level. Our advanced techniques will make your website the envy of your competitors. Reasonable prices are what makes us favored. High quality websites is what keeps us in the business. Visit our main website for more information.

## Internet Ads

You've built your website, but have you built your website traffic? We have provided several proven ways to get visitors to your website through this self-paced manual. However, don't stop there. If you really want to get noticed on the world wide web, be sure to visit our Internet Ads link on our main website. We have several websites which are being increasingly searched. Be certain to claim your spot in as many as you like. Inquire today.

## Web Resource

Lesley the Web Resource, LLC is a top resource for website owners. From website hosting to do-it-yourself and custom website design and development to Internet ads, we have what you need to begin or grow your Internet presence. Let us know how we can help you today.

# Resources

## *Internet Statistics*

1. Internet World Stats
http://www.internetworldstats.com/stats.htm

2. Low Cost ISPS
www.lowcost-isps.com

3. Alternative Search Engines
www.altsearchengines.com

## *Web Building, Web Advertising, and Web Traffic Resources*

www.DesignMyOwnWebPage.info

www.winfomaniac.com

www.GetFreeWebsiteTraffic.info

## *Marketing Materials*

www.CopyAndMail.com

# Resources (continued)

*Lesley the Web Resource, LLC*
website design and development
www.LesleyTheWebResource.com

*Lesley the Writer*
writing service
www.LesleyTheWriter.com

*Host Likely*SM
website hosting service
www.HostLikely.com

*True Multimedia*SM
www.TrueMM.com

# Another Useful Book

In this book, responsible website owners will uncover the following:

- 31 recommendations from a website consultant
- Resources from your guide, Dr. Webb
- To-the-point information
- Easy-to-follow format

Consult with this book at a fraction of the cost of a face-to-face consultation with your professional website designer / developer. Better yet, contact the website consultant who wrote this book to help you with your Preventative Website Maintenance Plan today.

## Another Useful Book

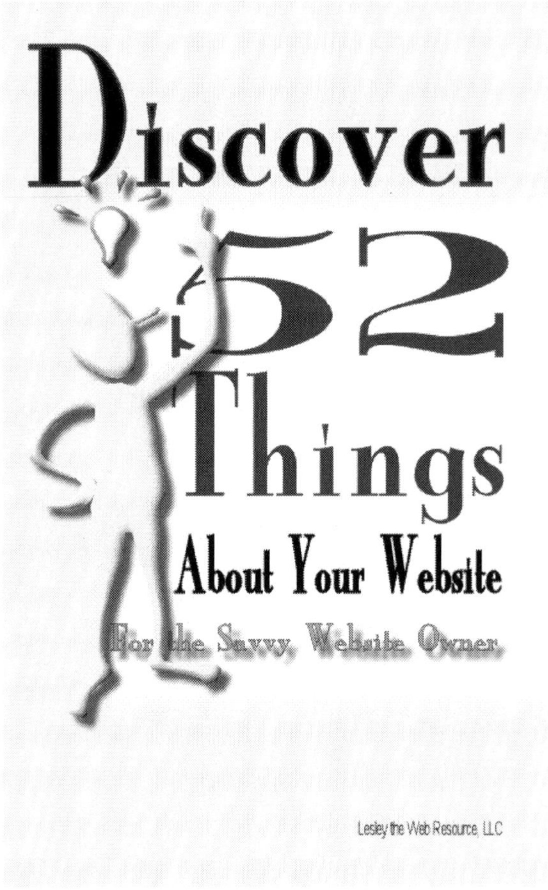


In this book, savvy website owners will uncover the following:

- 52 insider tips from a website consultant
- Time-saving resources
- To-the-point information
- Easy-to-follow format

Consult with this book at a fraction of the cost of a face-to-face consultation with your professional website designer / developer. Better yet, contact the website consultant who wrote this book to help you Discover More About Your Website today.

# Another Useful Book

In this book, smart website owners will uncover the following:

- 25 insider fixes from a website consultant
- Inspiring quotes from around the globe
- To-the-point information
- Easy-to-follow format

Consult with this book at a fraction of the cost of a face-to-face consultation with your professional website designer / developer. Better yet, contact the website consultant who wrote this book to help you Fix Minor (or Major) Website Boo-Boos today.

# Feedback

*Which Q.U.I.C.K. Fix Marketing solution would you like to read next?*

- ☐ *Another Q.U.I.C.K. Fix for Website Copywriting*
- ☐ *Another Q.U.I.C.K. Fix for Getting Website Visitors from Offline*
- ☐ *Another Q.U.I.C.K. Fix for Getting Website Visitors from the Internet*
- ☐ *Another Q.U.I.C.K. Fix for Basic Website Design*
- ☐ *Another suggestion*________________________________

# Let Us Keep You Updated

*When we have the occasional update, or when we produce the next Q.U.I.C.K. Fix, where would you like us to reach you? Mail your information to 4142 Ogletown-Stanton Rd. #442, Newark, Delaware 19713 or visit our website and use the Q.U.I.C.K. Fix link to send us your details via our secured web form:*

*Name:* ____________________________________

*Email:* ____________________________________

Made in United States
Orlando, FL
04 November 2026

90200406R00103